Knitted Toys

Jean Greenhowe

Knitted Toys

HAMLYN

Acknowledgements

The designs in this book were originally featured in WOMAN'S WEEKLY magazine and the author would like to express her thanks to the editor and the knitting department and home department staff, for their assistance and cooperation during the preparation of this book.

The author and publishers also wish to thank IPC Magazines Ltd, publishers of WOMAN'S WEEKLY, for their kind permission to reproduce their photographs.

The author's thanks are also due to BRUNSWICK YARNS, Brunswick Worsted Mills Inc, Pickens, S.C., USA, for generously providing samples of their knitting yarns.

This edition published in 1989
by The Hamlyn Publishing Group Limited,
part of Reed International Books,
Michelin House,
81 Fulham Road,
London SW3 6RB

ISBN 0 600 50286 4 (Hardback)
ISBN 0 600 56772 9 (Paperback)

Phototypeset in England by Servis Filmsetting Limited in 11 on 12 Apollo

Produced by Mandarin Offset
Printed in Hong Kong

Contents

Introduction

Knitted toys are colourful, cuddly and fun to make. They appeal to all ages, providing lovable, safe playthings for youngsters and attractive mascots for older children and adults. Most of the toys in this book can be made for next to nothing and the smallest of them requires only oddments of yarn.

There are full instructions for making well over 50 items, ranging from tiny toys which can be knitted in an instant to a 47 cm [$18\frac{1}{2}$ in] pair of dolls with sets of removable clothes. Most of the toys are worked in double knitting yarn which is widely available in a wonderful selection of colours. Only basic knitting skills are required because the knitted stitches and shapings are of the simplest kind, allowing even the inexperienced knitter to create attractive toys.

General instructions and useful tips

Safety first

Knitted toys are quite safe and suitable for young children so long as you do not add any potentially dangerous items such as wire, buttons or beads, which could become detached. On the other hand it would be perfectly safe to give an older child a toy which has beads or buttons sewn on for the eyes, so a little common sense should be used regarding the safety factor in toys. If in doubt it is always best to use felt for the eyes and noses or to embroider them with yarn.

Measurements

Any measurements in the instructions are given in metric, followed by the imperial equivalent in square brackets. Use whichever you wish.

USA knitting needles

Needle sizes are given in metric with the old UK sizes in square brackets. Use the following table to convert to the equivalent USA needle sizes.

The table only includes those needle sizes which are required to make the toys in this book.

Metric size	'Old' UK size	USA size
$2\frac{3}{4}$ mm	12	1
3 mm	11	2
$3\frac{1}{4}$ mm	10	3
$3\frac{3}{4}$ mm	9	4
4 mm	8	5
5 mm	6	7
$5\frac{1}{2}$ mm	5	8

Yarns

You will need only oddments of double knitting yarn to make the majority of the toy designs. Four ply yarn is required for making the knitted nursery rhyme scenes. You can use any make of yarn, no specific brands are mentioned.

***Opposite**: Two playful penguins, on the left the chef (page 54), on the right the penguin with snowballs (page 57)*

For some of the larger toys the amount of yarn required is quoted, to ensure that you have enough on hand to finish that part of the toy.

When particular colours are mentioned, this is either for authenticity [for example red yarn for Santa Claus] or to make sure that colours are changed when knitting different parts of the toy. You can of course work with whatever colours you have on hand.

When working in stripes of different colours it is not necessary to keep breaking and joining on the yarns. Simply carry each colour loosely up the side of the work, when it is required for the next stripe.

British and American knitting yarns

Only two types of British yarn are used for the toy designs in this book – double knitting and 4 ply. For knitters in the USA I have tested Brunswick Windrush [knitting worsted weight] and also Brunswick Fore-'n-Aft [sport weight] to check that they can be substituted for the British yarns.

Although the knitting worsted weight felt a little thicker than double knitting, both yarns knitted up in much the same way as the British equivalents, making little or no difference to the appearance of the finished toys.

Knitters in the USA should therefore use knitting worsted weight instead of double knitting and sport weight instead of 4 ply.

Tension

When knitting a garment which has to be made to fit a particular size, you must always take care that your tension is exactly the same as recommended in the knitting instructions.

However you don't need to be so precise when knitting toys. Your creation will be just as lovable even if it does turn out a bit larger or smaller than the size stated on the pattern.

The following tension chart is therefore intended as a *general* guide only, not to be followed slavishly, but to indicate that if you work near to these tensions then your toy will be more or less the same size as given in the pattern. If your tension varies, don't worry! Just make sure that your knitting is not so loose as to allow the stuffing to escape between the stitches. Should this happen, then use a smaller size knitting needle.

Tension chart

[measured over stocking stitch and before stuffing]

Working with 4 ply yarn:
3 mm [No 11] needles – 30 sts to 10 cm [4 in]

Working with double knitting yarn
$3\frac{1}{4}$ mm [No 10] needles – 25 sts to 10 cm [4 in]
3 mm [No 11] needles – 26 sts to 10 cm [4 in]

Working with double knitting yarn, used double:
$5\frac{1}{2}$ mm [No 5] needles – 16 sts to 10 cm [4 in]
5 mm [No 6] needles – 17 sts to 10 cm [4 in]

The making up instructions

In knitting patterns the directions for assembling the pieces normally come at the end, when all the knitting is completed. However, when making toys there can be so many bits and pieces that it is sometimes easier and less confusing to do the making up as the work progresses. Consequently, for some of the designs, the making up instructions follow after each piece is knitted.

A list of useful equipment

Knitters' sewing needles

These are usually available in two sizes for use with fine and heavy weight yarns. They have large eyes and smooth rounded points designed to pass between the knitted stitches when sewing up your work.

Other needles

You will find darning needles and ordinary sewing needles useful. The darning needle for passing yarn through a toy to work the mouth stitches and features, and the sewing needles for use with ordinary sewing threads.

Pins

Large glass-headed pins are the best kind to use when making knitted toys since they are so easy to see and to handle. For safety's sake, use a limited number of pins and count them from time to time to make sure that you haven't left any in the toy when sewing it up.

Sewing threads
If you don't have a stock of sewing threads in a variety of colours you can buy economical packs of tiny reels which are ideal for hand-sewing, each reel holding about 10 m [10 yd] of thread.

Tweezers
A pair of tweezers with pointed ends are extremely useful for turning small pieces right side out and for pushing small amounts of stuffing inside. Use them also to hold felt eyes and noses while spreading with adhesive and to position any such pieces on the toy.

Leather punch
This is not essential but if you have one then use it to punch out tiny felt circles for the eyes of the smallest toys.

Ruler or tape measure
Either metric or imperial will do.

Casting on and off

The first row after casting on is usually the right side of the work unless otherwise stated.

When casting on and off and also when joining on different colours, always leave a long end of yarn which can be used when making up the toy, to sew up each different coloured portion.

If the instructions say to cast on or cast off 'loosely', use a larger size of knitting needle to do this evenly.

The knitted stitches

Only two types of knitted stitch are used for the toys in this book; stocking stitch, where you knit one row and purl the next, and garter stitch, where you knit on every row.

Joining on new balls of yarn

Instead of knotting on the yarn at the beginning of a row, join on a fresh ball in the following way. Thread a darning needle with the new yarn then take the needle point through the yarn loop of the first stitch on the previous row and also through the yarn strand coming away from the first stitch on the needle, as

How to join on a new ball of yarn

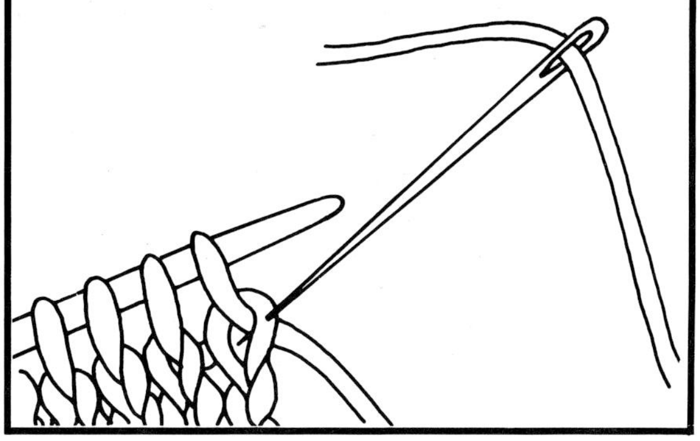

shown in the diagram. Pull the yarn through, leaving a long end. You must take care to pierce both the yarn loop and the yarn strand, then the first knitted stitch on your next row will hold firm and not slip open as you work.

The knitted shapes

When making knitted toys it is important to remember that the knitted pieces will stretch to shape when stuffed, so don't be put off by the unattractive appearance of the pieces at the knitting stage.

Making up the toy

Do not press any part of the work unless the instructions say so. Unless other instructions are given, join the seams with the wrong side of the work outside. Usually the main knitted pieces of the toy should be seamed by back-stitching or stab-stitching the row ends together, working one full stitch within each knitted edge. Always use matching yarn when sewing these seams.

To sew up those toys which are knitted with two strands of double knitting yarn together, use a single strand of yarn.

When adding any extra pieces to a knitted toy, such as felt pieces, knitted arms and hats, sew them in place with matching sewing thread instead of knitting yarn. This gives a really neat finish to the work. Alternatively you can split the yarn into single strands and use this instead.

Some knitted pieces need to be seamed by

oversewing the edges together instead of back-stitching and this is always mentioned in the instructions.

Stuffing the toy

Many types of stuffing are available for toy-making but man-made fibre fillings are the most suitable for knitted toys because they are washable. These fillings come in several grades ranging from the dearest high bulk white polyester to a dense multi-coloured and less expensive filling. The high bulk polyester is ideal for knitted toys since it goes further than the cheaper fillings and also makes beautifully soft resilient toys. Avoid kapok, which can not be washed, and foam chips which are lumpy and also highly inflammable.

Very small amounts of stuffing are required for making most of the toys, so the actual quantity is only quoted in the patterns for the larger toys.

When stuffing your toy, let the knitted fabric stretch naturally to shape and fill all parts evenly. Do not force more stuffing in than necessary. After filling, the toy should still be soft and yielding to the touch, yet firm enough to spring back to shape again.

Ladder stitch

This stitch is used to close the opening left on the toy after it has been stuffed. The edges of the opening are 'laced' together following the same line of vertical knitted stitches as in the back-stitched seam.

Using yarn to match the knitted fabric, secure it at one end of the opening. Now take a small straight stitch on one side of the opening then on the other. Continue working stitches alternately on each side then pull the yarn tight to bring the open edges together as shown in the diagram. For clarity the diagram is simplified to show only the ladder stitches.

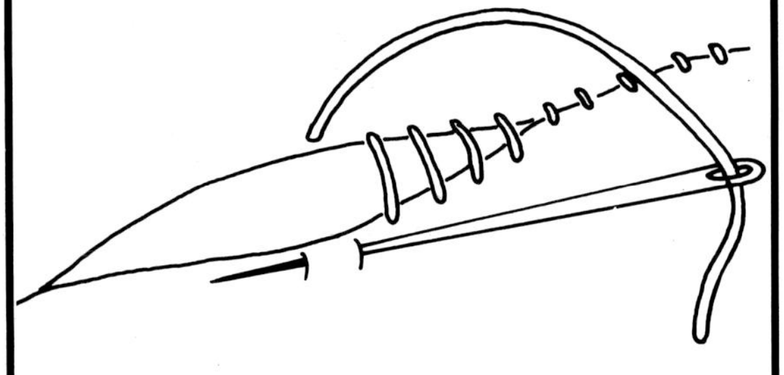

Ladder stitch

You can also use this stitch to attach the arms or legs of a toy to the body, forming an invisible join.

To shape the neck of a toy with a strand of yarn

When this is mentioned in the instructions use matching yarn and do it in the following way. Take the ends of the strand from the back to the front of the toy, cross them over and take to back again. Cross them over again and pull very tightly, then knot securely. Now use a darning needle to pass the ends of the yarn through the body at the position of the knot. Pull the darning needle through and snip off ends of yarn close to the body so that they disappear into the stuffing.

This method makes a really firm neck, compressing the stuffing tightly at this point and at the same time rounding off the head and shoulders. Shape the wrists in the same way if the instructions say so.

Felt pieces

Patterns for facial features and other felt pieces are printed full size for tracing directly off the pages. Trace them onto thin writing paper then cut out the patterns. You will only need very small scraps of felt in various colours.

Adhesive

Use an all-purpose clear adhesive such as UHU to stick the felt pieces to the toy. Before cutting out the felt pieces first spread the back of the felt with adhesive, work it into the felt with the fingertips, then leave to dry. When felt is treated in this way your cut out shapes will have smooth well-defined edges. The cut

Opposite from left to right: *Cinderella (page 67), snowman (page 65), footballer (page 65), Santa Claus (page 66) and Robin Hood (page 63)*

edges of ribbons, trimmings and braid can also be spread with a little adhesive, to prevent fraying. You can remove unwanted smears of UHU with a little acetone. Take care when using acetone as it is highly flammable.

To cut out tiny felt pieces, stick your paper pattern to the glued side of the felt with a dab of adhesive then cut out level with the edge of the paper pattern. Peel off the pattern before the adhesive dries completely.

Making a face

For a child-like appearance the eyes should always be placed half way down the face, if you position them higher your toy will have a more adult look. Indications for the placing of facial features may be given in the making up instructions, do follow these if you wish your toy to look like the one shown in the illustration.

To make sure that the eyes are level on a knitted toy, simply check that they are both in line with the same row of knitted stitches.

To work embroidered features

When the head of a toy is to be covered by the hair or a hat then the strand of yarn used for embroidering, for instance, the mouth can be started and finished off at the top or back of the head where it will be hidden. If the stitches can not be covered then proceed as follows. Thread a needle and knot the end of the yarn. Take the needle through the toy from the back of the head or body, passing it *between* the knitted stitches and bringing it out at the position required. Pull the yarn to draw the knotted end right inside the toy and tug, to make sure that the knot is caught in the stuffing. If the knot pulls right through the toy, try again at another position.

Now work the embroidered stitches as required, then pass the needle back through the toy to come out again at a position *between* the knitted stitches. Pass the needle back again between the *same* knitted stitches to come out at a different position. Repeat if necessary until the yarn is securely fastened off then snip off end of yarn. Take care to always pass the needle between the knitted stitches. If you split a stitch then the yarn strand will show on the surface of the toy.

To colour the cheeks

Dolls only seem to come to life after their cheeks are coloured and you should use a red drawing pencil for this. First, try rubbing the knitted stitches with the *side* of the pencil lead using a circular motion. This works very well on most yarns. If it doesn't work then moisten the pencil lead and apply a little colour to the centre of the cheek. Now use a bit of wet fabric to blend the colour into the surrounding knitted stitches.

The colour will come off if the toy is washed but it can, of course, be applied again.

To make a twisted yarn cord

Twisted cords are useful for decoration and making little bows where a knitted piece would be too bulky.

To make a cord from a single strand of yarn proceed as follows. First cut a length of yarn, three times as long as the measurement you will require. Knot one end round a door knob and make a loop in the other end to fit loosely over the index finger of your right hand. Now keeping the yarn taut, twist your finger round and round in a clockwise direction, steadying the yarn by holding your left hand cupped around it close to your right hand. Keep twisting until when relaxed, the strand of yarn begins to curl back tightly on itself. Now fold the strand in half, keeping it taut and bringing the ends together. Stroke along the length to make it curl up evenly. Knot both ends of the cord, trimming it to the required length.

To make a cord using two or more strands, use the same method, starting off with the specified number of strands.

To make a pom-pon

The usual way to make a pom-pon is to wind yarn round two card circles with holes cut in the centres. Here is another method which will not make such a dense pom-pon as with the card circles but is quicker and less fiddly.

For a small pom-pon, about 2 cm [$\frac{3}{4}$ in] in diameter, wind yarn about 30 times round two fingers. Pull the loops off your fingers and cut through twice so that you have 60 approximately equal lengths of yarn. Now knot a strand of matching yarn very tightly round the centre of the strands. Grip the long strands of yarn close to the knot then use sharp scissors to clip the strands to even lengths all over. Use the long strands to sew the pom-pon in place.

To make larger pom-pons wind yarn more times round three or four fingers.

Glossary for USA knitters

UK	USA
Cast off	Bind off
Tension	Gauge
Stocking stitch	Stockinette stitch
Snap fasteners	Snaps
Shirring elastic	Elastic thread

Abbreviations

These are the same for all the designs and should be read before working.

K	knit
P	purl
st[s]	stitch[es]
tog	together
inc	increase [by working twice into the same stitch]
dec	decrease [by working two stitches together]
st-st	stocking stitch [K on the right side, P on the wrong side]
g-st	garter stitch [K on every row]
( )	instructions which appear in round brackets are to be worked the number of times stated after the closing bracket
[ ]	square brackets contain the imperial measurement conversions, the old UK knitting needle sizes and also any special instructions
single rib	K 1 and P 1 alternately, on every row
*	
**	
***	a single asterisk, or group of two or more, is used to mark a place in the instructions which will be referred to later on. Meanwhile, work the row, following the instructions in the usual way
m	metre[s]
cm	centimetre[s]
mm	millimetre[s]
g	gram[s]
[in]	inch or inches
[yd]	yard or yards
[oz]	ounce or ounces

Twin dressing-up dolls – instructions begin on page 20

The toys

Twin dressing-up dolls

These super-sized boy and girl dolls, each 47 cm [18½ in] tall, come complete with removeable sets of clothes. There are jackets, caps, scarves and mittens, plus a pinafore dress for the girl and dungarees for the boy.

Their one-piece undergarments, socks and shoes are all knitted in as part of the basic doll with added ribbed bands at the neck, upper arms and legs. The underwear also serves as a short sleeved sweater underneath the pinafore dress and dungarees. In addition there is a jump suit and flower-trimmed dress for the girl and track suit, pants and jerkin for the boy.

You will need: A pair of 3 mm [No 11] knitting needles and double knitting yarn which is listed under separate headings for the dolls and their clothes, for quick reference.

Abbreviations: See page 17.

For each doll: Two 20 g balls of pale pink; two 20 g balls of white for the girl or pale blue for the boy; small ball of black for the shoes; 20 g ball of brushed yellow for the girl's hair, or brown for the boy; 150 g [5 oz] of stuffing; scraps of dark brown felt for the eyes; red and orange yarn for the mouth and nose stitches; a red pencil; adhesive.

For the girl's pinafore dress, scarf and hair ribbons: Three 20 g balls of green and oddment of yellow for scarf fringe; two buttons; two snap fasteners; shirring elastic.

For the boy's dungarees and scarf: Four 20 g balls of blue and oddment of red for scarf fringe; two buttons; two snap fasteners; shirring elastic.

For the jacket [the same for boy or girl]: Three 20 g balls of red for the girl or yellow for the boy; five buttons; five snap fasteners; oddments of yarn for knitting the snowman picture on back of the jacket as shown in the illustration.

For the mittens [the same for boy or girl]: Oddment of green for girl or blue for boy.

For the cap [the same for boy or girl]: Oddments of yarn to make stripes, as shown in the illustration.

For the girl's jump suit: Three 20 g balls of orange and oddment of white for the contrast bands; a 10 cm [4 in] long orange zip fastener; a small buckle for the belt.

For the boy's track suit: Four 20 g balls of blue and oddment of yellow for the contrast bands; a 25 cm [10 in] long blue open-ended zip fastener [as this is the shortest length available in this type of zip, it will have to be cut to length when sewing it to the jacket]; shirring elastic.

For the girl's flower-trimmed dress: Two 20 g balls of lilac; oddments of yellow and white; two small buttons.

For the boy's sleeveless jerkin: One 25 g ball of tweedy yarn; a 4½ mm [No 7] crochet hook [optional].

For the boy's trousers: Three 25 g balls of tan; a pair of 2¾ mm [No 12] knitting needles [which are required for the hems and waist edge of this garment only]; shirring elastic.

To make the doll

The head [make two pieces, both alike]

Begin at neck edge and using pink, cast on 12 sts.

1st row: Inc K wise into every st – 24 sts.

Next row: P.

Continue in st-st increasing 1 st at each end of next and every following alternate row until there are 34 sts.

St-st 31 rows.

Next row: (K 1, K 2 tog) to last st, K 1 – 23 sts.

Next row: P.

Next row: K 1, (K 2 tog) to end – 12 sts.

Cast off.

The body [make two pieces, both alike]

Begin at lower edge and using white or blue cast on 28 sts.

St-st 16 rows.

Dec 1 st at each end of next row – 26 sts.

St-st 5 rows.

Dec 1 st at each end of next row – 24 sts.

St-st 15 rows.

Shape shoulders: Cast off 2 sts at beginning of next 6 rows – 12 sts.

Cast off.

The arms [make two alike]

Begin at top of arm and using white or blue cast on 6 sts.

Work in st-st increasing 1 st at each end of every row until there are 26 sts.

St-st 8 rows.

Break off white or blue and join on pink then st-st 20 rows.

To shape wrist: Dec 1 st at each end of next row – 24 sts.

St-st 3 rows.

To shape hand: ** Inc 1 st at each end of next row – 26 sts.

St-st 3 rows.

Inc 1 st at each end of next row – 28 sts.

St-st 3 rows.

To shape thumb: Dec 1 st at each end of next row – 26 sts.

Next row: P.

Cast off 3 sts at beginning of next 2 rows – 20 sts.

St-st 4 rows.

Next row: (K 2 tog) to end – 10 sts.

P 1 row then cast off.

The legs [make two alike]

Begin at top of leg and using pink cast on 28 sts.

St-st 44 rows.

Break off pink and join on white or blue for sock.

St-st 10 rows.

Shape for foot: K 10, inc in next 8 sts, K to end – 36 sts.

* *Next row:* P.

Next row: K 10, inc in next st, K to last 12 sts, inc in next st, K to end * – 38 sts.

Break off white or blue and join on black for the shoe.

Continue shaping foot by repeating from * to * six times – 50 sts.

Cast off.

The foot soles [make two alike]

Begin at back of sole and using black cast on 4 sts.

Work in st-st increasing 1 st at each end of first and every following alternate row until there are 10 sts.

St-st 11 rows.

Inc 1 st at each end of next row – 12 sts.

St-st 9 rows.

Dec 1 st at each end of next row – 10 sts.

P 1 row.

Cast off 2 sts at beginning of next 2 rows – 6 sts.

Cast off.

The ears [for boy doll only, make two alike]

Using pink cast on 3 sts.

Work in st-st and inc 1 st at each end of first row – 5 sts.

St-st 3 rows, then inc 1 st at each end of next row – 7 sts.

St-st 3 rows, then dec 1 st at each end of next row – 5 sts.

Cast off.

To make up either doll

Join row ends of head pieces leaving cast on and cast off edges open. Join row ends of body pieces leaving cast on and cast off edges open.

Now join body and head together at neck edges [cast on edges of head and cast off edges of body]. Turn right side out and stuff head then gather round the cast off sts at top of head, pull up tightly and fasten off. Stuff body then catch lower cast on edges together at the exact centres.

Fold each leg in half and join row ends leaving cast on and cast off edges open. Sew foot soles in position placing cast on edges of soles to seam in each leg. Turn legs right side out and stuff, then sew open top edges of legs to lower edges of body having leg seams at centre back. Press seams around foot soles with a warm iron and a damp cloth.

Fold each arm in half and join row ends and round hands leaving top shaped edges open. Turn right side out and stuff, then sew open edges to each side of body having cast on edges of arms 2 cm [$\frac{3}{4}$in] down from doll's neck.

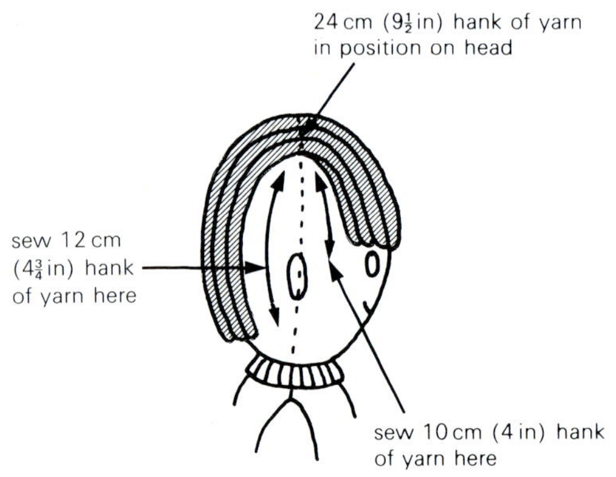

How to make boy's hair

For each doll work bands in single rib to match body colour as follows:

Neckband: Cast on 34 sts and work 3 rows then cast off loosely in rib. Place the band round doll's neck and oversew row ends at back then sew band to neck.

Sock tops: Cast on 32 sts and work 7 rows then cast off loosely in rib. Place bands round tops of doll's socks, oversew row ends at back then sew bands to socks.

Sleeve bands: Cast on 30 sts and work 3 rows then cast off loosely in rib. Sew to sleeves as for sock tops.

Leg tops: Cast on 32 sts and work 3 rows then cast off loosely in rib. Sew round tops of legs as for sock tops.

Make two short twisted cords from a single strand of red yarn, tie each in a small bow and sew to front of girl's shoes.

To work facial features [girl and boy alike]

Work a short stitch in orange yarn for nose 5.5 cm [2$\frac{1}{4}$in] up from the neck. Cut the eyes from brown felt using the pattern and stick them to face 3.5 cm [1$\frac{3}{8}$in] apart on either side of the nose as shown in the illustration.

Work a shallow W-shape 2 cm [$\frac{3}{4}$in] below nose for the mouth.

Colour the cheeks with red pencil.

For the boy, fold the ears having right side outside and oversew the row ends together. Sew the folded edges to each side of the head having lower edges of ears level with the mouth.

To make the girl's hair

First of all make the fringe by sewing loops of yarn to the top of the head seam, to hang down the forehead just above the eyes. Snip ends of loops evenly above the eyes.

Cut remainder of the yarn into 50 cm [20 in] lengths. Back stitch centre of the lengths to the position of the centre parting on doll's head from forehead to just above neck at back. Gather strands to each side of head and sew to the head seam level with the mouth. Plait the strands and trim ends evenly, tying round a strand of yarn to hold in place.

To make the boy's hair

Wind yarn 30 times round a 24 cm [$9\frac{1}{2}$ in] length of card. Slip wound lengths off the card and place this hank over the top of doll's head as shown in the diagram. Pin, then sew looped ends across forehead just above the eyes. In the same way, sew the other looped ends across back of head above neck. Sew the strands of yarn to the head at seam line at top of head also.

To cover the head at each side of face in front of each ear, wind yarn 10 times round a

10 cm [4 in] length of card. Sew looped ends to head to fill in the gaps as shown in diagram.

To cover the head at back behind each ear, wind yarn 20 times round a 12 cm [$4\frac{3}{4}$ in] length of card. Sew looped ends to head to fill in gaps as shown in diagram.

The clothes

To make the girl's pinafore dress

Skirt
Begin at hem edge of skirt and cast on 96 sts then g-st 4 rows.

St-st 28 rows.

Dec for waist: *Next row:* (K 1, K 2 tog) to end – 64 sts.

G-st 4 rows then cast off.

Bib
Cast on 18 sts.

1st row: K.

2nd row: K 3, P 12, K 3.

Repeat these 2 rows 7 more times.

G-st 5 rows then cast off.

Straps [make two alike]
Cast on 36 sts and g-st 4 rows then cast off.

To make up pinafore dress
Thread three rows of elastic through back of g-st rows at waist edge. Sew the cast on edge of bib just inside waist edge of skirt at centre. Join row ends of skirt.

Sew one end of each strap to back of skirt waist edge having ends of straps about 5 cm [2 in] apart. Sew snap fasteners to other ends of straps and also to inside of bib at top corners. Sew buttons to these corners on outside of bib.

To make the scarf [same for girl or boy]

Cast on 12 sts and work in g-st for 46 cm [18 in]. Cast off.

Add fringe to each end of scarf.

To make hair ribbons

For each one cast on 50 sts then cast off.

To make the jacket [same for girl or boy]

Back
Cast on 42 sts and g-st 4 rows.

St-st 24 rows.

To shape armholes: Cast off 4 sts at beginning of next 2 rows – 34 sts.

Now dec 1 st at each end of next and every following alternate row until 14 sts remain.

G-st 4 rows then cast off.

Right front
Cast on 23 sts and g-st 4 rows.

Next row: K.

Next row: P 19, K 4.

Repeat these 2 rows 11 more times.

Next row: K.

Shape armhole: *Next row:* Cast off 4 sts, P to last 4 sts, K 4 – 19 sts.

Continue working the 4 g-st border at the unshaped edge on every row, at the same time dec 1 st at end of next and every following alternate row until 9 sts remain.

G-st 4 rows then cast off.

Left front
Cast on 23 sts and g-st 4 rows.

Next row: K.

Next row: K 4, P 19.

Repeat these 2 rows 11 more times.

Shape armhole: *Next row:* Cast off 4 sts, K to end – 19 sts.

Next row: K 4, P to end.

Continue working the 4 g-st border at the unshaped edge on every row, at the same time dec 1 st at beginning of next and every following alternate row until 9 sts remain.

G-st 4 rows then cast off.

Sleeves [make two alike]
Cast on 36 sts and g-st 4 rows.

St-st 22 rows.

Shape top: Cast off 4 sts at beginning of next 2 rows – 28 sts. Now dec 1 st at each end of next and every following alternate row until 8 sts remain.

G-st 4 rows then cast off.

Jacket back decoration
For the snowman use white and cast on 10 sts.

St-st 14 rows.

To shape neck: Dec 1 st at each end of next row – 8 sts.

Next row: P.
Inc 1 st at each end of next row – 10 sts.
St-st 5 rows then dec 1 st at each end of next row – 8 sts.
Break off white and join on black for hat.
St-st 8 rows then cast off.

To finish off: Using black yarn, work eyes and mouth on the snowman's face in small stitches. Work a small orange stitch for nose. Sew the snowman to the jacket back having the cast on edge just above the g-st lower edge of jacket. Work a line of black stitches along lower edge of hat extending on either side for the hat brim.

Use brown yarn to work a broomstick as shown in the illustration. Use contrasting yarn to work a scarf in chain stitches.

Use white yarn to work stitches for snowflakes all over jacket back. Work a line of white back stitches underneath the snowman, for the ground, as illustrated on page 23.

Pockets [make two alike]
Cast on 12 sts and g-st 16 rows then cast off.

To make up the jacket
Sew pockets to fronts. Join armhole edges of sleeves to armhole edges of fronts and back. Join row ends of sleeves and side edges of fronts and back. Sew five snap fasteners to front g-st borders spacing them out evenly. Sew buttons over fasteners.

To make the cap [same for girl or boy]

Cast on 80 sts and work 4 rows in single rib.
St-st 30 rows, working in two row strips of available colours.
Keeping continuity of stripes correct, shape top of cap as follows:
1st row: (K 8, K 2 tog) to end – 72 sts.
2nd and every alternate row: P.
3rd row: (K 7, K 2 tog) to end – 64 sts.
5th row: (K 6, K 2 tog) to end – 56 sts.
7th row: (K 5, K 2 tog) to end – 48 sts.
9th row: (K 4, K 2 tog) to end – 40 sts.
11th row: (K 2, K 3 tog) to end –24 sts.
13th row: (K 3, tog) to end – 8 sts.
14th row: P.
Break off yarn leaving a long end, thread it through remaining sts, then pull up tightly and fasten off. Join row ends of cap then make a tassle and sew it to the top.

To make the mittens [same for girl or boy]

Cast on 24 sts and work 4 rows in single rib.
Work in st-st as for the doll's arm from ** (page 21) to the end. Join seams as for the arms. Make a twisted cord from a single strand of yarn making cord about 32 cm [$12\frac{1}{2}$ in] in length. Sew a mitten to each end of cord. Thread cord through jacket sleeves before putting jacket on doll.

To make the boy's dungarees [make two pieces alike]

Cast on 54 sts and g-st 4 rows.
St-st 44 rows.

Shape crotch: Cast off 3 sts at beginning of next 2 rows – 48 sts.
Now dec 1 st at each end of next 4 rows – 40 sts.
St-st 14 rows.

Dec for waist: *Next row:* (K 3, K 2 tog) to end – 32 sts.
G-st 4 rows then cast off.
Make the bib and straps as given for the girl's pinafore. [See opposite.]

To make up the dungarees
Thread elastic through g-st at waist edge as for girl's pinafore. Join the dungaree pieces to each other at the shaped crotch edges. Now join the row ends of each leg. Sew bib and straps in place etc. as for girl's pinafore.

To make the girl's jump suit

Legs and body [make two alike, each knitted in one piece]
** Using white begin at lower edge of leg and cast on 50 sts.
Work 4 rows in single rib. Break off white and join on orange.
Beginning with a K row, st-st 48 rows.

To shape the crotch: Cast off 2 sts at beginning of the next 2 rows, then dec 1 st at each end of the following 4 rows – 38 sts. **.
St-st 24 rows.

To shape the armholes: *Next row:* K 14, cast off 10 sts, K to end. Work on the last group of

14 sts and beginning with a P row, st-st 18 rows.

*** To shape the neck:** Cast off 4 sts at beginning of next and the following alternate row – 6 sts. Work 1 row then cast off remaining 6 sts for the shoulder edge. *

With wrong side of work facing, rejoin yarn to remaining group of 14 sts and beginning with a P row, st-st 17 rows.

To shape the neck: Work as for the other neck shaping from * to *.

Sleeves [make two alike]
Using white cast on 40 sts and work 4 rows in single rib.

Break off white and join on orange then st-st 10 rows.

To shape the top: Cast off 6 sts at beginning of next 2 rows, then dec 1 st at each end of the next 8 rows – 12 sts.

Cast off.

Belt
Using white cast on 70 sts. Work 5 rows in single rib, or as many rows as required to suit the size of the centre bar on the buckle.

Cast off in rib.

To make up the jump suit
Join the row ends of each leg as far as crotch shaping. Join row ends of one crotch seam from crotch shaping to neck edge. Join the curved portion of the remaining crotch seam, leaving 10 cm [4 in] of remainder of seam open for inserting the zip fastener.

Join cast off shoulder sts of each piece. Join row ends of each sleeve as far as top shaping. Sew top shaped portions of sleeves into the armholes, placing cast off sts of sleeves against cast off sts of armhole shaping.

For the neckband, pick up and K 40 sts round the neck edge. Work 4 rows in single rib then cast off in rib. Sew the zip fastener in place below the neckband. Sew one end of belt to the centre bar of the buckle.

***Opposite: top left**: Girl's jumpsuit (page 25); **top right**: Boy's tracksuit (page 27); **bottom left:** Girl's flower-trimmed dress (page 28); **bottom right**: Boy's sleeveless jerkin and matching trousers (page 28)*

To make the boy's track suit

Trouser legs [make two alike]
Work as given for the girl's jump suit from ** to **, using yellow yarn instead of white and blue instead of orange.

St-st 12 rows then work 4 rows in single rib. Cast off in rib.

Jacket body [worked in one piece up to armholes]
Using yellow cast on 78 sts and work 4 rows in single rib. Break off yellow and join on blue.

Beginning with a K row, st-st 20 rows.

To shape the armholes: *Next row:* K 14, [these sts are for the right front], cast off 10 sts, K 29 [these sts are for the back], cast off 10 sts, K to end [these sts are for the left front].

Work on left front sts first and beginning with a P row, st-st 18 rows.

Shape the neck: * Cast off 4 sts at beginning of the next and the following alternate row – 6 sts. Work 1 row, then cast off remaining 6 sts for shoulder edge. *

With wrong side of work facing, rejoin yarn to group of 30 sts for the back. Beginning with a P row, st-st 17 rows.

Shape the neck: *Next row:* K 10, cast off 10 sts, K to end. Work on last group of 10 sts for the left back neck and shoulder.

Next row: P.

Next row: Cast off 4 sts, K to end. Work 1 row, then cast off remaining 6 sts for shoulder edge.

With wrong side of work facing, rejoin yarn to group of 10 sts for right back neck and shoulder.

Next row: Cast off 4 sts, P to end. Work 1 row, then cast off remaining 6 sts for shoulder edge.

With wrong side of work facing, rejoin yarn to remaining group of 14 sts, for the right front. Beginning with a P row, st-st 17 rows.

Shape neck as for left front from * to *.

Sleeves [make two alike]
Using yellow cast on 40 sts and work 4 rows in single rib. Break off yellow and join on blue then st-st 28 rows.

To shape the top: Cast off 6 sts at beginning of next 2 rows, then dec 1 st at each end of next 8 rows – 12 sts. Cast off.

To make up the track suit
Join row ends of trouser pieces to each other at shaped crotch edges, then join row ends of each leg piece. Thread three rows of shirring elastic through wrong side of waistband.

Join cast off shoulder sts of jacket fronts to back. Join row ends of each sleeve as far as top shaping. Sew top shaped portion of sleeves into armholes, placing cast off sts of sleeves against cast off sts of armholes.

For the neckband, using yellow pick up and K 40 sts round the neck edge. Work 4 rows in single rib then cast off in rib. Open the zip fastener, separating the two sides. Trim a piece off each one at the top so that remainder will fit the jacket fronts from lower edge to beneath the neckband. Take care not to let the slide fastener slip off at this point. Now oversew around and between the zipper teeth at the cut top edges so that the slide fastener will stop at the top when zipped up. Sew the zip in place.

To make the flower-trimmed dress

[knitted in one piece up to the armholes]

Using lilac cast on 96 sts and g-st 4 rows. Beginning with a K row, st-st 37 rows.

To shape the armholes: *Next row:* P 20, cast off 8 sts, P 39, cast off 8 sts, P to end.

Work on the last group of 20 sts first.

* St-st 2 rows.

Next row: (K 2 tog) to end – 10 sts. G-st 4 rows then cast off.*

Rejoin yarn to next group of 40 sts and st-st 2 rows.

Next row: (K 2 tog) to end – 20 sts. G-st 4 rows then cast off.

Rejoin yarn to last group of 20 and work from * to *.

The neck frill
Using lilac cast on 120 sts and g-st 4 rows. St-st 6 rows.

Next row: (K 2 tog) to end – 60 sts. Cast off knitwise.

The flowers [make ten]
Using yellow cast on 4 sts.

Next row: Inc K wise into every st – 8 sts.

Next row: Inc K wise into every st – 16 sts. Cast off very loosely.

To make up the dress
Join row ends of dress from lower edge, leaving 5 cm [2 in] open at top of seam for the back opening. Sew cast off sts at centre of neck frill to the 20 cast off sts of dress front. Sew cast off sts at ends of frill to the 10 cast off sts of each back. Sew row ends of frill to the back opening edges. Sew two buttons to frill at one edge of back opening, then make yarn loops on opposite edge to fasten around the buttons.

Join row ends of each flower and work a few white stitches at centre of each one. Sew flowers at regular intervals round edge of dress.

To make the boy's sleeveless jerkin

Work as given for the track suit body using the tweed yarn throughout. [See page 27.]

To make up the jerkin
Join cast off shoulder sts of fronts to back. If desired, work a row of double crochet round front, neck edges and armhole edges.

To make the boy's trousers

Trouser legs [make two alike]
Begin at lower edge of leg and using $2\frac{3}{4}$ mm [No 12] needles, cast on 50 sts.

Beginning with a K row, st-st 3 rows then change to 3 mm [No 11] needles and K 1 row.

Next row: K 12, slip next st onto right hand needle, K 24, slip next st onto right hand needle, K 12.

Next row: P.

Repeat these last 2 rows 25 more times.

Now continue slipping the 2 sts as on the previous K rows and shape the crotch as follows: cast off 2 sts at beginning of the next 2 rows then dec 1 st at each end of the following 4 rows – 38 sts.

St-st 17 rows then K the next row.

Change to $2\frac{3}{4}$ mm [No 12] needles and g-st 3 rows. Cast off.

To make up the trousers
Join row ends of the pieces to each other at the shaped crotch edges. Join row ends of each leg by oversewing neatly. Turn in the waist edge at the K row and catch cast off edge in place on the inside. Thread a row of double shirring elastic through the waist edge.

Cuddly clown

This colourful clown, complete with jaunty umbrella, is about 30 cm [12 in] tall. His stripy jumper, trousers and shoes are all knitted as part of him.

You will need: Oddments of double knitting yarn in assorted colours as shown in the illustration; a pair of $3\frac{1}{4}$ mm [No 10] knitting needles; small amount of stuffing; scraps of red and black felt; a red pencil; adhesive.

Abbreviations: See page 17.

The body

Begin at lower edge of one leg and using yellow cast on 22 sts.

St-st 22 rows then break off yarn and leave sts on a spare needle.

Work another leg in the same way, then with right side of work facing, K across both sets of leg sts – 44 sts.

St-st 9 rows.

Break off yellow and join on dark blue and light blue.

Continue in st-st, working 16 rows in two row stripes beginning with dark blue then light blue.

Keeping sequence of stripes correct, shape neck: *Next row:* K 7, K 2 tog, K 4, K 2 tog, K 14, K 2 tog, K 4, K 2 tog, K 7 – 40 sts.

St-st 3 rows.

Break off the blue yarns and join on cream for the head.

St-st 2 rows.

To shape head: *Next row:* K 7, inc in next st, K 4, inc in next st, K 14, inc in next st, K 4, inc in next st, K 7 – 44 sts.

St-st 25 rows.

Next row: (K 2 tog) to end – 22 sts.

Break off yarn leaving a long end then thread it through remaining sts and leave.

The arms [make two alike]

Begin at lower edge of arm and using cream cast on 8 sts.

Next row: Inc K wise into every st – 16 sts.

Beginning with a P row, st-st 9 rows.

Break off cream, join on dark blue and st-st 4 rows.

FULL SIZE PATTERNS

Break off dark blue, join on light blue and st-st 14 rows.

Shape top of arm: Dec 1 st at each end of next 6 rows – 4 sts.

Cast off.

The shoes [make two alike]

Using green cast on 6 sts.

Work in st-st, inc 1 st at each end of next 2 rows – 10 sts. St-st 4 rows, then inc 1 st at each end of next row – 12 sts.

St-st 9 rows.

Next row: K 3, inc in next 6 sts, K 3 – 18 sts.

St-st 7 rows.

Next row: (K 2 tog) 3 times, K 6, (K 2 tog) 3 times – 12 sts.

Next row: P.

Dec 1 st at each end of the next row – 10 sts.

Next row: P.

Break off green and join on black for shoe sole.

St-st 26 rows.

Dec 1 st at each end of next 2 rows – 6 sts.

Cast off.

The shoe bows [make two alike]

Using red cast on 12 sts and g-st 8 rows.

Cast off.

The hair

Using yellow cast on 46 sts.

1st row: K 1; * insert right hand needle K wise into next st, place first two fingers of left hand at back of st, then wind yarn anti-clockwise round needle and fingers 3 times, then round tip of right hand needle only, draw through the 4 loops; repeat from * until 1 st remains; K 1.

2nd row: K 1; * K 4 tog pulling loops down firmly as you go; repeat from * to last st; K 1.

Cast off.

The hat

The hat brim

Using green cast on 46 sts and K 1 row.

Next row: Inc K wise into every st – 92 sts.

G-st 4 rows then cast off.

The hat crown

Using green cast on 60 sts and g-st 22 rows.

Cast off.

The hat top

Using green cast on 64 sts and g-st 5 rows.

Next row: (K 2 tog) to end – 32 sts.

G-st 4 rows.

Next row: (K 2 tog) to end – 16 sts.

G-st 3 rows.

Next row: (K 2 tog) to end – 8 sts.

G-st 2 rows.

Next row: (K 2 tog) to end – 4 sts.

Break off yarn leaving a long end then thread it through remaining sts, pull up tightly and fasten off.

The hat band

Using red cast on 50 sts and g-st 4 rows.

Cast off.

The hat flowers

[make one blue, one white and one yellow]

Cast on 4 sts.

Next row: Inc K wise into every st – 8 sts.

Next row: K.

Next row: Inc K wise into every st – 16 sts.

G-st 2 rows then cast off loosely.

The braces [make two alike]

Using red cast on 40 sts and g-st 4 rows.

Cast off.

The buttons [make four alike]

Using green cast on 8 sts.

Next row: Inc K wise into every st – 16 sts.

Cast off loosely.

The neck bow

Using yellow cast on 10 sts and g-st 6 rows.

Cast off.

The knee patches [make two alike]

Using blue cast on 6 sts and st-st 6 rows.

Cast off.

The umbrella handle

Using green cast on 24 sts and g-st 4 rows.

Cast off.

The umbrella top

Using red cast on 6 sts.

Next row: Inc K wise into every st – 12 sts.

Work 16 rows in single rib.

Next row: Inc K wise into every st – 24 sts.

K 1 row then cast off.

To make up

Join row ends of legs then row ends of body and head. Turn right side out and stuff through lower edges of legs and top of head. Pull up length of yarn at top of head tightly and fasten off. Shape neck by tying a length of yarn tightly round lower edge of head. Sew ends into body.

Join row ends of arms and round hands leaving shaped top edges open. Turn and stuff then sew open top edges of arms to sides of body 1 cm [$\frac{3}{8}$ in] down from neck.

Bring cast on and cast off edges of each shoe together and join down sides. Turn shoes right side out and stuff, then ladder stitch the opening. Sew shoes underneath open edges of legs as shown in the illustration having cast on and cast off edges of shoes at backs of legs. Tie a length of yarn tightly round centre of each shoe bow then sew bows to shoes as illustrated.

Work small stitches on wrong side of knee patches in white, then sew patches to knees.

Place braces over shoulders crossing them over at back then sew ends of braces to trousers. Join row ends of each button to form a

circle then work a cross stitch in white at centre of each one. Sew buttons in place, lapping them over ends of braces as shown in the illustration.

Tie a length of yarn round centre of neck bow then sew bow under chin.

For the mouth, work a 1 cm [$\frac{3}{8}$ in] long stitch in red yarn 2.5 cm [1 in] above the neck. Cut the eyes from black felt using the pattern then glue them in place 1.5 cm [$\frac{5}{8}$ in] above mouth and 2 cm [$\frac{3}{4}$ in] apart. Work a small blue horizontal stitch at each side of each eye as shown in illustration.

Cut the nose from red felt using the pattern and stick it between the eyes.

Colour the cheeks with red pencil.

Join row ends of the hair and place it on the head so that the loops are above the neck at the back, rising to above the eyes at the front. Sew the top edge of hair to the head.

Join row ends of hat brim then sew the inner edge to the head to cover the top edge of the hair. Join row ends of the hat crown piece. Join row ends of the hat top piece. Sew hat top to the crown, then sew lower edge of crown to the hat brim on the head.

Join row ends of the hat band then catch it to the hat all round lower edge of the crown.

Join row ends of each flower then work a few stitches in contrast colour yarn at centre of each flower. Sew flowers to hat as illustrated.

Oversew cast on and cast off edges of the umbrella handle together, pulling up stitches tightly at one end to form the curved handle. Join row ends of the umbrella top then push handle through. Stuff umbrella top, keeping the handle at centre, then tie a length of yarn tightly round at top of the single rib. Finally, sew the umbrella handle to the clown's hand.

Knit a nursery rhyme

Three popular nursery rhymes in the shape of little pastoral scenes, all knitted in 4 ply yarn. Boy Blue, Mary and her little lamb and Miss Muffet each measure about 11.5 m [4½ in] in height. You can sew the dolls in place to make charming decorations for a child's room, or leave them free for extra play value.

You will need: Oddments of 4 ply yarn in assorted colours as shown in the illustrations; a pair of 3 mm [No 11] knitting needles; small amount of stuffing; tiny guipure flower trimming; a short length of silver gift cord for Miss Muffet's spoon; a red pencil.

Abbreviations: See page 17.

Notes: Use the illustrations as a guide to the colours used. Particular colours of yarn are only mentioned in the instructions when necessary, e.g. white for Mary's lamb, green for the grassy banks.

When sewing up the items, split the yarn into two 2 ply strands and use one strand only. Join all the seams by oversewing the edges together instead of back stitching.

The looped pattern: The hedgerows around each scene and the haycock are all knitted in a two row looped pattern which is given here to avoid repetition throughout the instructions.

Cast on the required number of sts as stated in the individual instructions.

1st row: K 1; * insert right hand needle K wise into next st, place first finger of left hand at back of st, wind yarn anti-clockwise round needle and finger 4 times then round tip of right hand needle only, draw through the 5 loops; repeat from * until 1 st remains; K 1.

2nd row: K 1; * K 5 tog, pulling the loops down firmly as you go; repeat from * until 1 st remains; K 1.

Little Miss Muffet

Grassy bank

Using two strands of green in different shades, cast on 14 sts.

1st row: Inc K wise into every st – 28 sts.
Work in g-st until work measures 10 cm [4 in].

Next row: (K 2 tog) to end – 14 sts. Cast off.

Fold 4 cm [1½ in] under at one side edge of the work and sew it in place while at the same time pushing in stuffing to make the raised 'tuffet' at the back of the bank.

Side hedgerows

Make two pieces alike one for each side of the grassy bank, as follows.

Using green cast on 16 sts and work the two row looped pattern 4 times. Cast off.

Back hedgerow

For the piece at the back of the grassy bank, cast on 16 sts and work the two row looped pattern 6 times. Cast off.

Oversew the cast on and cast off edges of each hedgerow piece together then sew hedgerows to sides and back of bank, catching the row ends together at the corners where they meet each other.

Legs and body

Begin at the ankle edge of one leg and using white or other suitable colour for stockings cast on 4 sts.

1st row: Inc K wise into every st – 8 sts.

Now beginning with a P row, work 15 rows in st-st. Leave sts on a safety pin. Work second leg in the same way, then with right side of work facing, K across 8 sts of second leg then 8 sts of first leg – 16 sts.

St-st 7 rows. Break off yarn and join on colour for top of body. St-st 8 rows. Break off yarn and join on pink for the head then st-st 10 rows.

Next row: (K 2 tog) to end – 8 sts.

Break off yarn leaving a long end then thread it loosely through remaining sts.

Join row ends of each leg then join body and head seam leaving top of head open.

Turn right side out. Stuff legs leaving a small gap in stuffing at tops of legs so that they will bend, then stuff body and head. Pull up yarn tightly at top of head and fasten off. Tie a strand of yarn tightly round neck then sew ends of yarn into body.

Arms [make two alike]

Begin at hand and using pink cast on 3 sts.

1st row: Inc K wise into every st – 6 sts.

Beginning with a P row, st-st 3 rows. Break off pink and join on yarn to match top of body. St-st 14 rows then cast off loosely.

Join row ends leaving cast off edges open. Turn right side out and stuff, then tie a strand of yarn round each wrist as for neck.

Sew the open top edges of arms to each side of body 2 rows below neck. Bend arms at the elbows as shown in the illustration and catch in place at the bends.

Shoes [make two alike]

Begin at top edge of shoe and cast on 13 sts.

1st row: K 5, inc in next 3 sts, K 5 – 16 sts.

Next row: P. Break off yarn and join on contrast colour for shoe sole.

Next row: K 5, (K 2 tog) 3 times, K 5 – 13 sts. Cast off.

Join row ends and cast off edges of shoes leaving cast on edges open. Turn right side out, stuff toes of shoes, then push shoes onto ends of legs and sew top edges to legs.

Face and hair

Work the facial features slightly to one side of the head so that Miss Muffet will appear to be turning to look at the spider.

Use double red yarn for the mouth and work a single vertical stitch 2 knitted rows above the neck. Work a small black stitch at centre of mouth. Use black yarn for the eyes and work a single chain stitch for each eye, 2 knitted stitches apart and 1 knitted row above the mouth. Colour cheeks with red pencil.

For the hair, split a few 15 cm [6 in] lengths of yellow yarn into single strands. Sew centre of strands to top of head then sew strands in bunches to each side of head. Trim ends of hair evenly. Remainder of the head will be covered by the hat.

Little Miss Muffet (page 33)

Hat

Cast on 44 sts and g-st 2 rows. Beginning with a K row, st-st 2 rows.

* *Next row:* (K 2 tog) to end – 22 sts. Join on contrast yarn for hat band and beginning with a P row st-st 2 rows. Break off contrast yarn and continue in hat colour, st-st 5 rows.

Next row: (K 2 tog) to end – 11 sts.

Break off yarn leaving a long end, thread through remaining sts, then pull up tightly and fasten off. Press the hat brim with a warm iron. Oversew row ends together. Place hat on head and sew it to head through the row knitted before the hat band rows.

Skirt and bodice

Begin at hem edge of skirt and cast on 36 sts. G-st 2 rows.

Beginning with a K row, st-st 10 rows.

Next row: (K 2 tog) to end – 18 sts. Break off skirt colour and join on contrast yarn for bodice.

Beginning with a P row st-st 6 rows. Cast off loosely.

Sew 3 small horizontal contrast colour stitches down centre front of bodice and take

Little Boy Blue (page 36)

Mary had a little lamb (page 37)

small running stitches round lower edge of skirt as shown in illustration. Join row ends of skirt and bodice and put on doll having cast off edge of bodice under the arms. Use double yarn in the bodice colour to work a stitch over each shoulder from front to back, for the shoulder straps.

Spoon

Cut a 10 cm [5 in] length of silver gift wrapping cord. Make it into a twisted cord and knot the ends together. Trim off the ends of cord close to the knot then press the knot to flatten it and form the bowl of the spoon. The spoon should be about 2 cm [$\frac{3}{4}$ in] long. Use tweezers to pass the spoon through Miss Muffet's hand then catch it in place with sewing thread.

Bowl

Cast on 14 sts and st-st 4 rows. Break off yarn leaving a long end. Thread it through sts and pull up tightly then fasten off. Join row ends of work then turn bowl right side out. Tease out a strand of cream coloured yarn and sew into bowl using sewing thread.

Sew the bowl to Miss Muffet's hand then sew it to her skirt where it touches.

Spider

Using dark brown cast on 4 sts for the body.

1st row: Inc K wise into every st – 8 sts.

Beginning with a P row, st-st 6 rows.

Next row: (P 2 tog) to end – 4 sts.

Cast off.

Gather round edge of knitting and pull up gathers tightly enclosing a little stuffing then fasten off. Work 2 small white stitches for eyes. Sew the centres of four 5 cm [2 in] lengths of dark brown yarn underneath body for the legs. If desired, put a dab of adhesive on the end of each leg and roll between your finger and thumb to prevent the yarn from fraying out. Trim the ends of the legs.

To assemble the scene

Place Miss Muffet in position on the grassy bank. Sew skirt and shoes in place where they touch the bank. Using yellow yarn sew a few guipure flowers to the bank taking stitches through their centres. Sew the spider in place if desired.

Little Boy Blue

The field

Begin at front edge and using one strand of yellow together with one strand of pale green, cast on 24 sts.

Work in g-st, inc 1 st at each end of every row until there are 36 sts. Continue in g-st until work measures 11 cm [$4\frac{1}{2}$ in] from the beginning. Cast off.

Hedgerow

Using green cast on 75 sts. Work the two row looped pattern once, then cast off. Oversew the cast off edge to the sides and back of the field. Spread out the loops and catch to field here and there where they touch.

Make another hedgerow piece in the same way and oversew the cast off edge to the cast off edge of the first piece.

Haycock

Using yellow cast on 28 sts. Work the two row looped pattern once.

Now continue working the two row pattern and at the same time dec 1 st at each end of the next and every alternate row until 10 sts remain. Break off yarn leaving a long end and thread it through remaining sts, pull up tightly and fasten off.

Join row ends of work, back stitching seam to bring loops together and pulling stitches tightly to shorten this edge slightly. Turn right side out and stuff, then sew lower edge of haycock to a corner of the field.

Legs, body and shoes

Make these as for Miss Muffet using shades of blue as shown in the illustration on page 34.

Jacket body

Begin at lower edge and using blue to match the legs cast on 26 sts.

G-st 2 rows.

Next row: K.

Next row: K 2, P to last 2 sts, K 2.

Repeat the last two rows 5 more times.

Next row: K.2, (K 2 tog) to last 2 sts, K 2 – 15 sts.

Break off yarn leaving a long end and thread it through remaining sts. Place this edge round doll's neck and pull up yarn length tightly, catching row end sts together at centre front. Sew a small yarn bow to neck at front.

Arms

Make as for Miss Muffet using blue to match jacket body. Sew tops of arms to each side of jacket taking stitches through jacket and into body.

Face and hair

Work a small red stitch for mouth and small V-shapes for the eyes in black and referring to Miss Muffet instructions on page 34 for placing the features etc. For the ears thread a darning needle with double pink yarn and work a small loop at each side of the head. For the hair thread a darning needle with brown yarn and work long vertical stitches above the forehead, in front of the ears and above the neck at back. Remainder of the head will be covered by the hat.

Hat

Using blue to match the jacket cast on 44 sts and g-st 2 rows. Now work as for Miss Muffet's hat from * to the end.

The horn

Using brown yarn cast on 4 sts. Beginning with a K row st-st 4 rows.

Next row: K, inc in first and last st – 6 sts.

St-st 6 rows then cast off.

Oversew row ends of work together pulling stitches tightly to make the horn curve. Turn right side out and stuff.

To assemble the scene

Sew Boy Blue and horn in position on the field as shown in the illustration, catching pants, shoes and hands to the field where they touch. Sew the hat to the haycock also.

Mary had a little lamb

Grassy bank and Mary

Make in the same way as for Miss Muffet using different colours of yarn as illustrated and making the mouth stitch as for Boy Blue.

Lamb's body

Begin at front end of the body and using white cast on 8 sts.

1st row: Inc K wise into every st – 16 sts.

Work 16 rows in g-st.

Next row: (K 2 tog) to end – 8 sts. Cast off.

Oversew row ends of work together then across cast off edge. Turn right side out and stuff, then oversew the opening.

Head

Using white cast on 12 sts and work 10 rows g-st.

Next row: (K 2 tog) to end – 6 sts.

Next row: (K 2 tog) to end – 3 sts.

Break off yarn leaving a long end, thread it through remaining sts then pull up tightly and fasten off. Oversew row ends of work together then turn right side out. Bring seam to centre back of head then stuff head and oversew cast on edges to close. Sew back of head to front of body, turning it slightly to one side. Work the eyes as for Miss Muffet, then work a small black stitch for the mouth and a pink stitch for the nose as illustrated on page 35.

Ears [make two alike]

Using black cast on 4 sts and K 1 row.

Next row: (P 2 tog) twice – 2 sts.

Next row: K 2 tog and fasten off.

Sew cast on edges of ears to sides of head as illustrated on page 35.

Legs [make four alike]

Note that P side of the white portion of the legs is the right side. Begin at top of leg and using white cast on 5 sts.

Beginning with a K row, st-st 4 rows. Break off white and join on black.

Next row: P.

Next row: K. Break off yarn leaving a long end. Thread it through sts, pull up tightly and fasten off then oversew row ends of work together. Turn right side out and stuff, then sew open ends of legs underneath body at the front and back.

Tail

Note that P side of work is the right side. Using white cast on 4 sts and beginning with a K row, st-st 10 rows. Break off yarn leaving a long end. Thread it through sts, pull up tightly and fasten off. Oversew row ends of work together having right side outside, then sew cast on edge of tail to back of lamb.
Make a twisted cord from a single strand of yarn and tie in a bow round lamb's neck.

To assemble the scene

Sew Mary and lamb to the grassy bank as for Miss Muffet.

Knit a car

Knit up a super sports car or two in double knitting yarn. There are two versions, the smallest measuring 10 cm [4 in] in length. The larger car, using two strands of yarn together, measures about 16.5 cm [6½ in].

The small sports car

You will need: Oddments of double knitting yarn in assorted colours as shown in the illustration; a pair of 3 mm [No 11] knitting needles; small amount of stuffing; red and black embroidery thread [or you can use several strands of ordinary sewing thread instead].

Abbreviations: See page 17.

Note: Join all seams by oversewing edges together.

Main body of car

Begin at back of car and using red cast on 8 sts.

1st row: Inc K wise into every st – 16 sts.

Beginning with a P row, st-st 29 rows.

Break off red and join on black for the radiator grill, then st-st 4 rows.

Next row: (K 2 tog) to end – 8 sts.

Break off yarn leaving a long end, thread it through remaining sts then pull up tightly and fasten off.

Join row ends leaving cast on edges open. Turn right side out and stuff firmly then gather up cast on edge tightly and fasten off. Note that seam should be positioned underneath the car when assembling the pieces.

Now using white yarn, work five long vertical stitches up the front of the radiator grill.

Bumper strip

Using black cast on 58 sts then cast off.

Join row ends of strip then sew it round the car body close to the lower edge.

Wheels [make five alike]

Using yellow cast on 4 sts.

1st row: Inc K wise into every st – 8 sts.

2nd row: K.

3rd row: Inc K wise into every st – 16 sts.

G-st 2 rows then cast off loosely.

Join row ends of wheel to form a circle then work a few stitches in blue at centre of wheel. Sew four wheels to the car as shown in the illustration and lay the fifth one aside until later on.

Driver

Begin at lower edge of body and using green cast on 10 sts.

St-st 6 rows.

Break off green and join on white for the head.

St-st 6 rows.

Break off white and join on brown for the hair.

St-st 2 rows.

Next row: (K 2 tog) to end – 5 sts.

Break off yarn leaving a long end then thread it through remaining sts, pull up tightly and fasten off.

Join row ends leaving cast on edges open. Turn right side out and stuff. Tie a strand of white yarn tightly round to shape neck at first knitted row in white.

Plait six strands of brown yarn to make an 8 cm [3¼ in] length. Sew the plait to top and sides of head. If making a boy driver omit the plait.

For the eyes work a couple of small stitches in black embroidery thread and work a stitch in red for the mouth.

Knit the hat as given for the wheel using lilac yarn, but work an extra row of g-st before casting off. Work a few small stitches in yellow at top of the hat for a bobble.

For each arm cast on 8 sts using green, st-st 2 rows then cast off. Oversew cast on and cast off edges of each arm together.

To work the hand, thread a needle with white yarn and work oversewing stitches at the end of the arm to cover the green completely, as shown in the illustration. Sew the arms to the sides of the body below neck.

For the scarf cast on 26 sts using pink, then cast off. Put the scarf round the driver's neck and catch in place.

Sew the lower edge of the driver's body to centre top of car, placing front of body 4 cm [$1\frac{1}{2}$ in] away from the radiator grill.

Steering wheel

Using black cast on 7 sts.

1st row: Inc K wise into every st – 14 sts.

Cast off loosely.

Join row ends then work a cross stitch at centre of wheel in white. Place wheel in front of driver and sew it to lower edge of body at front then sew driver's hands to the wheel at each side.

Driver's compartment

Using red cast on 30 sts then g-st 4 rows and cast off.

Join row ends then pin cast on edge to top of car around the driver as shown in the illustration. Sew this edge in place. Sew steering wheel to the driver's compartment at front.

Now sew the fifth wheel to the back of the car.

Headlights [make two alike]

Using white cast on 8 sts then cast off loosely.

Join row ends then sew to car beside the radiator grill at the front.

Number plates [make one white and one yellow]

Cast on 6 sts then g-st 2 rows and cast off.

Using black thread work G 1 on the number plates for a girl driver or B 1 for a boy driver. Sew the plates to the bumper strip, the white one at the front and the yellow one at the back.

The large sports car

Make this in exactly the same way as for the small sports car, but use two strands of double knitting yarn throughout and work on $5\frac{1}{2}$ mm [No 5] knitting needles.

To make a girl driver for the large car, plait 12 strands of yarn to make a 13 cm [$5\frac{1}{2}$ in] length, for the hair.

Fairy tale toys

Snow White and her friends the seven dwarfs are so easy to make with oddments of brightly coloured double knitting yarn.

Each dwarf is knitted in light and dark shades of the same colour and they are numbered one to seven. Children will enjoy learning to identify the colours and the numbers.

Snow White measures 28 cm [11 in] tall, while the smallest dwarf is 20 cm [8 in], excluding his hat. They come complete with their sacks of gold and silver nuggets.

For the dwarfs you will need: Oddments of double knitting yarn in light and dark shades of – red, yellow, green, blue, purple, brown and pink; oddments of yellow and brown for hair, braces, belts and sacks; pale pink for faces and hands; black for eyes and boots; small amount of white 4 ply yarn for numbers 1 to 7; for belt buckles, buttons and nuggets, small amount of Twilleys gold and silver Goldfingering yarn [or for an inexpensive alternative you can use gift wrapping cord or ordinary double knitting yarn]; a pair of 3 mm [No 11] knitting needles; 350 g [12 oz] of stuffing [enough to make all seven dwarfs]; a red pencil.

For Snow White you will need: One 20 g ball of double knitting yarn in white and one in yellow; two 20 g balls of blue; oddments of dark blue, pale blue, pale pink and red; a pair of 3 mm [No 11] knitting needles; small amount of stuffing; a red pencil.

Abbreviations: See page 17.

The dwarfs

Notes: The dwarfs are worked in three sizes – short and fat, short and thin, and tall and thin.

In the instructions Dk means dark shade of the colour and Lt means light shade of the same colour.

Brown yarn is used for the braces and belts. Goldfingering [or alternative as already mentioned], is used for the buckles and buttons.

4 ply yarn is used for the numbers *only*.

Refer to the instructions for each individual dwarf before working from the basic instructions and note that additional details are also given in individual instructions.

Basic instructions for the thin dwarf

Instructions which follow are for two sizes – short, and a little taller.

Body

Begin at lower edge of one boot and using black cast on 14 sts.

1st row: Inc K wise into every st – 28 sts.

Beginning with a K row st-st 10 rows.

Shape top of boot: *Next row:* K 4, (K 2 tog) twice, (K 3 tog) 4 times, (K 2 tog) twice, K 4 – 16 sts.

Work 3 rows g-st.

Break off black and join on Lt **.

Beginning with a K row, st-st 12 rows for short dwarf, 14 rows for taller dwarf.

Break off yarn and leave sts on a spare needle then work another leg in the same way.

Now having right side of work facing K across the 16 sts already on needle, then K the 16 sts from spare needle – 32 sts.

St-st 7 rows.

Break off Lt and join on Dk then st-st 12 rows for short dwarf, 14 rows for taller dwarf.

To shape shoulders: *Next row:* (K 4, K 2 tog) twice, K 8, (K 2 tog, K 4) twice – 28 sts.

St-st 3 rows.

Break off Dk and join on pale pink for the head.

St-st 2 rows.

Shape head: *Next row:* K 6, (inc in next st, K 2) 5 times, inc in next st, K 6 – 34 sts.

St-st 25 rows.

Next row: (K 2 tog) to end – 17 sts.

Break off yarn leaving a long end then thread it loosely through remaining sts and leave.

Arms [make two alike]

Begin at hand and using pale pink cast on 7sts.

1st row: Inc K wise into every st – 14 sts.

Beginning with a K row, st-st 8 rows.
Break off pale pink and join on Dk.
St-st 6 rows for short dwarf, 8 rows for taller dwarf.

Shape elbow: *Next row:* K 12, turn,
Next row: P 10, turn.
Next row: K to end.
Now continue in st-st, working 7 rows for short dwarf, 9 rows for taller dwarf.

To shape top of arm: Dec 1 st at each end of next and every following row until 2 sts remain.
Cast off.

Basic instructions for short fat dwarf

Work as for thin dwarf as far as **.
Beginning with a K row, st-st 12 rows.
Break off yarn and leave sts on a spare needle then work another leg in the same way.
Now having right side of work facing K across the 16 sts already on needle, then the 16 sts from spare needle – 32 sts.
St-st 5 rows.

Shape body: *Next row:* K 5, inc in next st, (K 3, inc in next st) 5 times, K 6 – 38 sts.
Next row: P.
Break off Lt and join on Dk then st-st 12 rows.

To shape shoulders: *Next row:* (K 5, K 2 tog) twice, K 10, (K 2 tog, K 5) twice – 34 sts.
St-st 3 rows.
Break off Dk and join on pale pink for head then st-st 2 rows.

Shape head: *Next row:* K 9, inc in next st, (K 4, inc in next st) 3 times, K 9 – 38 sts.
St-st 25 rows.
Next row: (K 2 tog) to end – 19 sts.
Break off yarn leaving a long end then thread it loosely through remaining sts.

Arms [make two alike]
Make exactly as given for short thin dwarf.

Hat [the same for all the dwarfs]

Using Dk cast on 50 sts.
Work 4 rows in g-st.
Break off Dk and join on Lt then beginning with a K row, st-st 6 rows.

To shape top: Dec 1 st at each end of next and every following alternate row until 26 sts remain, then dec 1 st at each end of next and every following row until 4 sts remain.
Break off yarn leaving a long end. Thread it through remaining sts then pull up tightly and fasten off.

Scarf [the same for all the dwarfs]

Using Lt cast on 70 sts and g-st 5 rows then cast off.

To make up dwarfs

Body
Join row ends of work from head as far as joining row at top of legs. Now join row ends of each leg and round boot as far as cast on sts. Oversew cast on sts of boots together.
Turn body right side out and stuff boots, pushing out toe ends well, then stuff legs, body and finally head. Draw up the length of yarn at top of head and fasten off securely. Tie a strand of pale pink yarn tightly round neck then sew ends of yarn into body.

Arms
Join row ends of each arm leaving top shaped portion open. Oversew cast on sts at ends of hands together. Turn right side out and stuff. Sew open ends of arms to each side of body having cast off sts about 5 mm [$\frac{1}{4}$ in] away from neck. Tie a strand of Dk yarn round each wrist in same way as for neck.

Hat
Oversew row ends of hat together then turn right side out but do not sew hat to head at this stage.

Faces and hair

Nose
Using pale pink cast on 3 sts.
1st row: Inc K wise into every st – 6 sts.
St-st 5 rows.
Break off yarn leaving a long end and thread it through sts on needle. Colour right side of nose with red pencil then gather all round edges. Pull up gathers tightly enclosing a little stuffing then fasten off. Sew nose to face, varying the position for each dwarf as shown in the illustration on page 43.

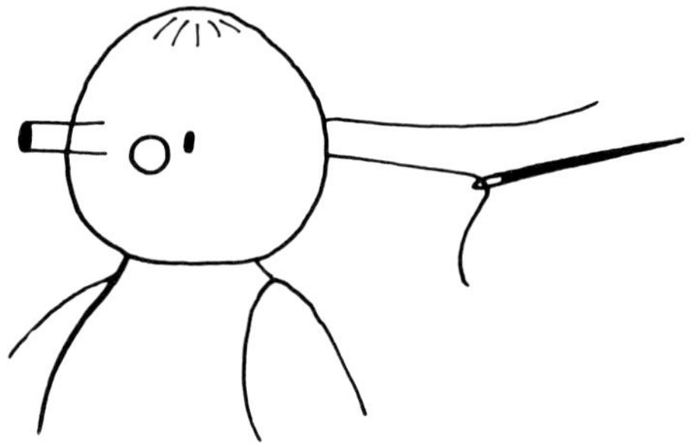

DWARF
How to sew yarn knots (for eyes) into head

Eyes [both alike]
For each eye cut a 40 cm [16 in] length of black yarn. At centre of each length tie a knot, but wrap yarn 6 or 8 times around [instead of once], before pulling knot tight.

Sew ends of yarn into head from face through to back of head as shown in diagram 1, then knot ends of yarn together at back of head for each eye, pulling yarn to depress eyes slightly into head. Vary positions of eyes for each dwarf. Add eyebrows if stated in individual instructions by working a small straight black stitch above each eye.

Mouth
Work a loose straight horizontal stitch for mouth below the nose using red yarn. Next, work a tiny vertical stitch below the first mouth line, taking it around first stitch to pull mouth into a V-shape. Vary length and position of first stitch for different facial expressions.

Cheeks
Colour cheeks with red pencil.

Hair [see also individual instructions]
Stuff top of hat lightly and pull hat onto head having seam at centre back above neck. Wind yellow or brown yarn a few times around one finger. Slip these loops inside hat at centre top. For some dwarfs make another two lots of loops and push these inside hat at each side [see illustration].

Sew cast on edge of hat to head all round catching hair in place at the same time. Bend pointed end of hat into various positions and catch to head to hold in place.

Individual dwarf instructions

Dwarf number 1

Make a tall thin dwarf, following basic instructions. Add hair at front of hat.

Tunic skirt
Using Dk cast on 50 sts and K 1 row.

Now beginning with a K row. St-st 7 rows.

Next row: P 3, (P 2 tog, P 5) 6 times, P 2 tog, P 3 – 43 sts.

Break off Dk and join on brown for belt.

G-st 5 rows then cast off.

To make up
Join row ends of belt only. Put tunic skirt on dwarf having the open edges at centre front and the cast off edge lapping the first row of Dk on body. Sew cast off edge to body.

Buckle
Using any of the yarns suggested, cast on 22 sts then cast off. Join row ends then sew buckle to centre front of belt as shown in the illustration.

The number one
Using white 4 ply cast on 10 sts then cast off. Sew to front of tunic.

Dwarf number 2

Make a short fat dwarf following basic instructions. Add eyebrows and omit hair.

Braces [make two alike]
Using brown cast on 36 sts, g-st 3 rows then cast off. Sew ends of braces in place on dwarf, lapping the ends 1 cm [$\frac{3}{8}$ in] over the Lt colour on the body and crossing the braces over at back. Catch braces to shoulders also.

Buttons [make four alike]
Using any of yarns suggested, cast on 10 sts then cast off. Join row ends then sew buttons to ends of braces.

The number two
Using white 4 ply cast on 20 sts then cast off. Use pins to form the number to shape on the dwarf then sew it in place.

Dwarf number 3

Make a short thin dwarf following basic instructions, adding hair at front of hat.

Belt

Using brown cast on 35 sts and g-st 3 rows then cast off.

Join row ends of belt then put it on the dwarf where the body colours join. Sew belt in place. Make buckle as for dwarf number 1.

The number 3

Using white 4 ply cast on 24 sts then cast off. Use pins to form the number to shape on the dwarf then sew it in place.

Dwarf number 4

Make as for number 2 adding hair at sides of hat and above face and omitting eyebrows.

The number 4
Using white 4 ply cast on 14 sts for main piece then cast off. For the small cross piece cast on 4 sts then cast off. Use pins to form the number to shape on the dwarf then sew it in place.

Dwarf number 5

Make exactly as for number 1, omitting the hair and adding eyebrows.

The number 5
Using white 4 ply cast on 20 sts then cast off. Use pins to form the number to shape on the dwarf then sew it in place.

Dwarf number 6

Make exactly as for dwarf number 3.

The number 6
Using white 4 ply cast on 18 sts then cast off. Use pins to form the number to shape on the dwarf then sew it in place.

Dwarf number 7

Make exactly as for dwarf number 4 adding eyebrows.

The number 7
Using white 4 ply cast on 14 sts then cast off. Use pins to form the number to shape on the dwarf then sew it in place.

The sacks of silver and gold nuggets

To make a sack
Using brown cast on 22 sts and g-st 2 rows.
Beginning with a K row, st-st 55 rows.
G-st 2 rows then cast off.
Bring cast on and cast off edges together having K side of work on the outside. Oversew the row ends together then turn sack right side out.

To make a gold or silver nugget
Using yarn suggested cast on 14 sts.
St-st 14 rows then cast off.
To vary sizes of nuggets cast on one or two less sts and work fewer or more rows.
To make up, fold nugget having K side on the inside and bringing row ends together. Oversew all round the edges leaving a gap for turning. Turn right side out and oversew gap. Now take stitches through the nugget several times, pulling yarn tightly each time, to make an irregular lumpy shape.
Fasten off the yarn.

Snow White

Right leg

Begin at lower edge of right shoe and using blue cast on 18 sts.
1st row: Inc K wise into every st – 36 sts.
Beginning with a K row st-st 8 rows.
Break off blue and join on white then st-st 2 rows **.
Next row: K 2, (K 3 tog) 8 times, K 10 – 20 sts.
St-st 29 rows.
Break off white and leave sts on a spare needle.

Left leg

Work as for right leg as far as **.
Next row: K 10, (K 3 tog) 8 times, K 2 – 20 sts.
St-st 29 rows.
Break off white and join on blue.

Body

With right side of work facing and using blue, K across the left leg sts then across the right leg sts on spare needle – 40 sts.
St-st 27 rows.
Shape shoulders: *Next row:* K 7, K 2 tog, K 2, K 2 tog, K 14, K 2 tog, K 2, K 2 tog, K 7 – 36 sts.
P 1 row.
Break off blue and join on white.
St-st 4 rows.
Shape neck: *Next row:* K 3, (K 2 tog, K 2) 7 times, K 2 tog, K 3 – 28 sts.
P 1 row.

Shape head: *Next row:* K 2, (inc in next st, K 1) 12 times, K 2 – 40 sts.

St-st 31 rows.

Next row: (K 2 tog) to end – 20 sts. Break off yarn leaving a long end then thread it loosely through remaining sts and leave.

Arms [make two alike]

Begin at hand and using white cast on 8 sts.

1st row: Inc K wise into every st – 16 sts.

Beginning with a K row, st-st 20 rows.

Shape elbow: *Next row:* K 14, turn.

Next row: P 12, turn.

Next row: K to end.

Now continue in st-st and work 9 rows. Break off white and join on blue and g-st 2 rows.

Shape for sleeve: *Next row:* K 1, (inc K wise into every st) to last st, K 1 – 30 sts.

Beginning with a P row, st-st 9 rows, decreasing 1 st at each end of every row – 12 sts.

Next row: (K 2 tog) to end – 6 sts.

Cast off.

Skirt

Using yellow cast on 80 sts and g-st 4 rows.

Now beginning with a K row, st-st 32 rows.

Shape waist: *Next row:* (K 2 tog) to end – 40 sts.

Cast off.

Collar

Using yellow cast on 30 sts.

1st row: Inc K wise into every st – 60 sts.

G-st 2 rows then cast off.

Bonnet

Using blue cast on 46 sts and g-st 4 rows.

Now beginning with a K row, st-st 16 rows.

Next row: K 10, (K 2 tog, K 1) 8 times, K 2 tog, K 10 – 37 sts.

P 1 row.

Next row: K 10, (K 2 tog, K 1) 5 times, K 2 tog, K 10 – 31 sts.

P 1 row.

Next row: K 10, (K 2 tog, K 1) 3 times, K 2 tog, K 10 – 27 sts.

Cast off.

To make up, fold bonnet bringing row ends together then oversew across cast off sts. With right side of work facing and using blue, pick up and K 28 sts along the edges of the row ends.

G-st 2 rows then cast off.

Apron

Using pale blue cast on 20 sts and g-st 2 rows.

Next row: K.

Next row: K 1, P 18, K 1.

Repeat these last 2 rows 9 more times.

Next row: (K 2 tog) to end – 10 sts.

Cast off.

For the waistband cut a 3 m (3 yd) length of pale blue yarn and make a twisted cord using yarn double. Sew cast off edge of apron to centre of waistband.

To make up Snow White

Body

Join row ends of work from head as far as the joining row at top of legs, leaving a gap in seam for stuffing. Now join row ends of each leg and round shoes as far as cast on sts.

Bring cast on sts of right shoe together having the leg seam in the position shown in diagram 2, then oversew across cast on sts.

Sew cast on sts of left shoe in same way, reversing position of leg seam.

Turn body right side out and stuff shoes, pushing out toe ends well, then stuff legs, body and finally head, inserting stuffing through back opening and through top of head. Pull up length of yarn at top of head and fasten off.

Ladder stitch back opening then tie a strand of white yarn tightly round neck and sew ends of yarn into body.

Arms

Join row ends of each arm leaving top shaped portion open. Oversew cast on sts at ends of hands together. Turn right side out and stuff. Sew open ends of arms to each side of body having cast off sts just below neck. Tie a strand of white yarn round each wrist as for neck, 8 rows away from cast on sts.

Shoe bows

Make a twisted cord for each shoe from a 1 m [1 yd] length of blue yarn. Sew centre of each cord to the back of each shoe at top, then tie cords in a bow at centre front. Trim ends of cord and knot. Catch the bows to feet.

Skirt

Work two rows of running stitches using red and blue yarn, along the g-st hem edge of skirt. Join row ends of skirt then put it on the doll with seam at centre back. Sew cast off edge of skirt to body, half way up.

Apron

Tie the apron round doll's waist and trim ends of cord to length then knot.

Sleeve decoration

Using red yarn, work a long vertical chain stitch at centre of each sleeve, then work a straight stitch at centre of chain stitch to fill it in.

Repeat this three times, on either side of first stitch, leaving 3 knitted sts between each one.

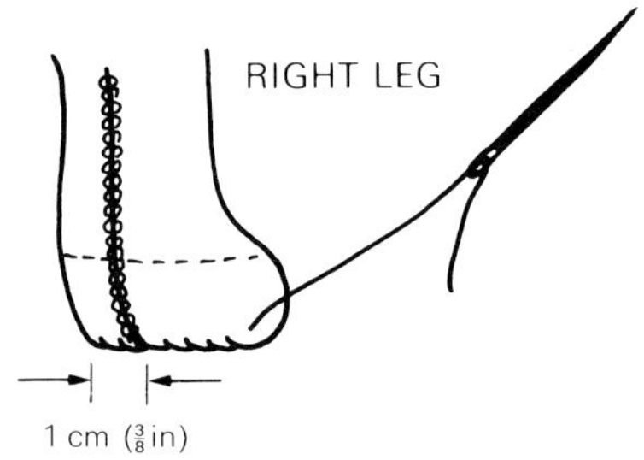

SNOW WHITE
How to oversew lower cast-on edges of right foot together

Collar

Sew cast on edge of collar round neck, level with blue on body and taking collar over the top edge of each sleeve. Join row ends of collar at centre back. Catch other edge of collar to doll through the first row of knitted sts.

Face

Make the eyes in the same way as for the dwarfs, using double dark blue yarn and winding yarn round four times before pulling the knot tight. Sew eyes to face as for dwarfs.

For the nose make a tiny knot using pale pink yarn and sew it in place as for eyes keeping knot in a horizontal position.

Make the mouth and colour cheeks as for dwarfs.

Hair and bonnet

Make two twisted cords as for the shoe cords and sew one to each side of the bonnet level with the picked up row of sts.

For the hair make a hank of black yarn by winding it ten times around a 33 cm [13 in] length of card. Take hank off the card and tie a strand of yarn round centre of hank.

Pin this tied centre to forehead about 4 cm [$1\frac{1}{2}$ in] in front of gathered top of head. Make a few short loops of black yarn and tuck them under pinned centre of hair, for the fringe. Sew loops and tied centre of hair to head. Take yarn strands down each side of face towards back of neck. Sew strands to each side of head.

Now put bonnet on doll just lapping cast on edge over hair, then tie cords in a bow under chin. Shorten cords as necessary then catch bow to neck. Sew bonnet to the head round the edges.

Five humpty-dumpty toys

Five roly-poly characters to knit up quickly using two strands of double knitting yarn. You can make Jack and Jill, Grandma and Grandpa and Hyacinth, the cuddliest fat fairy. Each one measures about 28 cm [11 in] from top to toe.

You will need: Oddments of double knitting yarn in assorted colours as shown in the illustrations; a pair of $5\frac{1}{2}$mm [No 5] knitting needles and a pair of $3\frac{3}{4}$mm [No 9] knitting needles; small amount of stuffing for each toy; scraps of felt for facial features; short lengths of narrow tape, braids, trimmings etc.

Abbreviations: See page 17.

Notes: Instructions are given for the basic shape of the toy followed by individual instructions with variations for each character. For a tweedy effect, use two different colours or shades of the yarn together.

Important note: Please remember that the double knitting yarn is to be used *double* throughout and worked on $5\frac{1}{2}$mm [No 5] knitting needles. This is taken for granted in the instructions for each piece and so will not be mentioned again.

When single yarn and $3\frac{3}{4}$mm [No 9] needles are required [for the looped fringes and Grandpa's eyebrows only] this will *always* be mentioned in the instructions.

Basic shape

The body

Begin at lower edge and using the desired colour for lower body cast on 6 sts loosely then work as follows.

1st row: Inc K wise into every st – 12 sts.

2nd row: P.

3rd row: Inc K wise into every st – 24 sts.

Beginning with a P row, st-st 3 rows.

Next row: Inc K wise into every st – 48 sts.

Continue in st-st and work 7 rows.

Centre body stripe: Break off lower body colour and join on contrast colour for centre body.

St-st 6 rows.

The head: Break off centre body colour and join on colour for head [cream, fawn or pink in the toys illustrated].

St-st 4 rows.

Next row: K 5, (K 2 tog, K 10) 3 times, K 2 tog, K 5 – 44 sts.

St-st 9 rows.

Next row: K 4, (K 2 tog, K 9) 3 times, K 2 tog, K 5 – 40 sts.

St-st 3 rows.

To shape top of head: *1st row:* (K 2, K 2 tog) to end – 30 sts.

2nd and every alternate row: P.

3rd row: (K 1, K 2 tog) to end – 20 sts.

5th row: (K 2 tog) to end – 10 sts.

7th row: (K 2 tog) to end – 5 sts.

Break off yarn leaving long ends, thread through remaining sts, then pull up tightly and fasten off.

The arms [make two alike]

Begin at top of arm and using the same colour as used for the centre body stripe, cast on 12 sts.

St-st 8 rows.

Break off yarn and join on yarn in same colour as used for head.

St-st 6 rows

Next row: (K 2 tog) to end – 6 sts.

Break off yarn and finish off as for top of head.

The legs [make two alike]

Begin at top of leg using the same colour as used for the lower body and cast on 14 sts.

St-st 16 rows.

Break off yarn and join on contrasting colour yarn for the shoe.

St-st 8 rows.

Next row: (K 2 tog) to end – 7 sts.

Break off yarn and finish off as for top of head.

To make up the basic shape

Gather up the cast on sts of body tightly and fasten off then join row ends of body leaving a small gap in head for turning. Turn right side out and stuff, then ladder stitch gap. Note that seam will be at centre back of toy.

Fold each arm and join the row ends leaving cast on edges open. Turn and stuff then oversew top edges together. Sew an arm to each side of body at position of centre stripe, taking care that the cast on edges of arms are in a vertical position [see illustrations].

Sew leg seams as for arms then turn right side out. Stuff lower portion of legs then stuff upper portion more lightly. Oversew top edges together having leg seams at centre back of legs. Sew legs to body at front having tops of legs in a horizontal position and two knitted rows up from last inc row at base of body.

Jack Humpty

Make the basic body, arms and legs.

The face

Using the patterns cut the eyes from blue felt, pupils from black felt, nose from red felt and cheeks from pink felt. Sew nose in place 3.5 cm [1¼ in] above centre body stripe. Sew pupils to eyes then sew eyes in place as illustrated.

Using single yarn work a small V-shape for mouth about 2 cm [¾ in] above centre body stripe, securing end of yarn under position of one felt cheek [where it will be hidden] and fastening off yarn under position of other cheek. Now sew cheeks in place.

The hair

For the hair, make the first row of looped fringe as follows.

Using single yarn and 3¾ mm [No 9] needles cast on 50 sts.

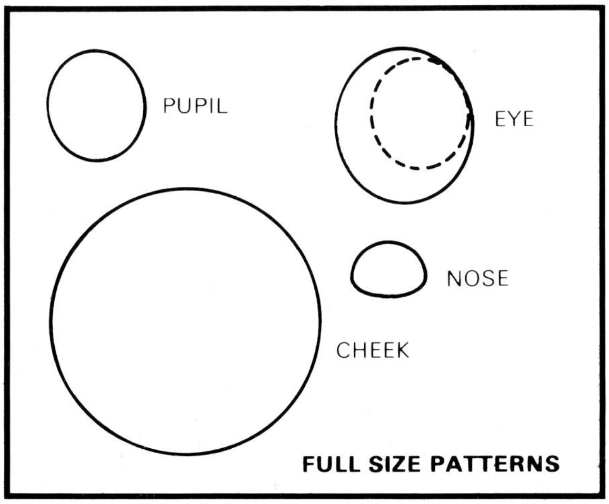

Next row: K 1; * insert right hand needle K wise into next st, place first two fingers of left hand at back of st then wind yarn anti-clockwise round needle and fingers 3 times then round tip of right hand needle only, draw through the 4 loops; repeat from * until 1 st remains; K 1.

Next row: K 1; * K 4 tog pulling loops down firmly as you go; repeat from * until 1 st remains; K 1 – 50 sts.

Cast off.

Join row ends of the looped fringe to form a circle.

Make three more fringes in the same way casting on 40 sts, 30 sts, and 10 sts. Sew all fringes to head, starting with the longest and ending with the 10 st fringe at the very top of head, to cover head completely.

Make a small bow from a twisted yarn cord and sew to front as illustrated.

Jill Humpty

Make the basic body, arms and legs then add facial features in same way as for Jack Humpty.

The hair

For the hair cut a ball of yarn into lengths about 50 cm [20 in] long. Sew a few loops of yarn to forehead for a fringe. Cut a 14 cm [5½ in] length of tape and stitch centres of the lengths of yarn to tape to cover it, within 1 cm [⅜ in] of each end of tape.

Turn under these ends of tape and place on head at position of centre parting having tape against head. Sew to head through stitched line on tape. Gather and sew yarn strands in a bunch at each side of head. Plait yarn strands then tie round bows made from twisted yarn cords. Trim ends of hair to even lengths.

The skirt fringe

Make this to match the centre body stripe colour.

Using single yarn and 3¾ mm [No 9] needles cast on 70 sts.

Work as for Jack's hair fringe but wind the

yarn round three fingers instead of two. Sew skirt round toy at lower end of centre body stripe.

Hyacinth Humpty the Fairy

Make the basic body shape working the lower body and the centre body stripe in the same colour.

Work the first 16 rows of the legs in the same colour as used for the head.

For the arms, after casting on, work 4 rows only in the centre body stripe colour and make remainder of arms in same colour as the head. Add facial features as for Jack. Sew braid or trimming round body and arms as illustrated.

The hair

Make this in same way as for Jill but trim ends of hair instead of plaiting.

The skirt fringe

Make in the same way as for Jill.

The head-dress

Work this in the same way as for Jack's first row of hair fringe, winding yarn round one finger instead of two. Sew to head as shown in the illustration.

Grandma Humpty

Make the basic body, arms and legs. Add nose, mouth and cheeks as for Jack. For the eyes cut and sew on black felt pupils only.

Sew trimming round body and arms as illustrated and add a twisted yarn bow to front.

The hair

Make this in the same way as for Jill but cut the yarn into 60 cm [24 in] lengths. After plaiting the yarn strands, coil the plaits round, tuck in the yarn ends, then sew plaits to head.

The skirt fringe

Make in the same way as for Jill.

Grandpa Humpty

Make the basic body, arms and legs and add facial features as for Grandma.

The hair

Make first row of hair fringe as for Jack but cast on 50 sts only. Sew this fringe round back of head from one side of the head to the other. Make a second row of hair fringe casting on 40 sts, then sew this in place just above first hair fringe.

The eyebrows [make two alike]

Using single yarn and $3\frac{3}{4}$ mm [No 9] needles cast on 5 sts.

G-st 2 rows then cast off. Sew in place above the eyes.

The moustache

Make this in the same looped pattern as for Jack's hair, casting on 6 sts, winding yarn round one finger and working first row of pattern only.

Break off yarn and thread it through all the sts then fasten off. Sew moustache under the nose.

The scarf

Cast on 3 sts and work in g-st for 46 cm [18 in] then cast off.

Sew scarf in place as shown in the illustration.

Playful penguins

Five little penguins just 11.5 cm [4½ in] high having fun in a winter wonderland, they have even made their very own snow penguin! These toys make ideal mascots for older children or adults.

For the basic penguins you will need: Oddments of double knitting yarn in black, white, yellow and orange; a pair of 3 mm [No 11] knitting needles; small amount of stuffing; two 6 mm [¼ in] diameter black shiny beads for each penguin's eyes.

Abbreviations: See page 17.

Notes: These toys are not suitable for very young children. To find the materials required for the penguins' accessories, refer to the individual instructions for each penguin.

Materials and instructions for the snow penguin are given at the end of all the other instructions.

To make the basic penguin

Body

Begin at lower edge and using black cast on 12 sts.

1st row: Inc K wise into every st – 24 sts.

Now beginning with a K row, work in st-st throughout.

Shape tail as follows: Inc in first two and last two sts on the next 3 rows – 36 sts.

P 1 row.

To complete tail shaping: Dec 1 st at each end of next 6 rows – 24 sts.

St-st 12 rows.

Shape neck: *Next row:* K 4, (K 2 tog) 8 times, K 4 – 16 sts.

P 1 row.

Shape head: *Next row:* K 4, (inc in next st) 8 times, K 4 – 24 sts.

St-st 13 rows.

Shape top of head: *Next row:* (K 2 tog) to end – 12 sts.

P 1 row.

Next row: (K 2 tog) to end – 6 sts.

Break off yarn leaving a long end then thread it loosely through remaining sts and leave.

To make up

Gather along the cast on sts of body, then pull up tightly and fasten off. Oversew row ends of tail, then body together, then turn right side out. Stuff, then pull up length of yarn tightly at top of head and fasten off.

Chest piece

Begin at lower edge and using white cast on 4 sts.

1st row: Inc K wise into every st – 8 sts.

2nd row: Inc K wise into every st – 16 sts.

Beginning with a P row, st-st 19 rows.

Next row: (K 2 tog) to end – 8 sts.

Cast off.

Sew the chest piece to front of penguin, having the cast off edge level with the neck shaping row.

Wings [make two alike]

Begin at upper edge and using black cast on 6 sts.

Beginning with a K row, st-st 14 rows.

Continue in st-st decreasing 1 st at each end of next 2 rows – 2 sts.

K 1 row.

Continue in st-st, increasing 1 st at each end of next row – 4 sts.

Break off black and join on white for inside of wing.

St-st 14 rows. Cast off.

To make up

Bring cast on and cast off edges together, then oversew row ends of wing together. Turn wing right side out then oversew cast on and cast off edges together. Then sew these edges to sides of penguin level with neck shaping row.

Feet [make two alike]

Using yellow cast on 3 sts.

1st row: Inc K wise into every st – 6 sts.

Beginning with a P row st-st 3 rows.

Next row: (K 2 tog, take yarn once around tip of right hand needle) twice, K 2 tog – 5 sts.

Keeping st-st correct, work 4 rows then cast off.

To make up

Oversew cast on and cast off edges together having right side of st-st outside. Sew these edges to front of penguin at lower edge of chest piece, having cast on edges against penguin and leaving a small space between the feet at centre front.

Eyes

See individual penguin instructions for positioning of eyes on the head, but sew all eyes in place as follows.

Using strong double sewing thread, sew on the beads by taking needle from one side of face through to the other, having 8 knitted sts between the beads. Pull thread tightly to depress beads into the head, then fasten off securely.

Beak

Using orange cast on 6 sts and K 1 row.

Continue in st-st decreasing 1 st at each end of next row – 4 sts.

St-st 1 row, then dec 1 st at each end of next row – 2 sts.

Break off yarn leaving a long end then thread it through remaining sts and fasten off.

To make up

Oversew row ends of beak together having right side of st-st outside. Push a little stuffing in beak. Tidy up any loose knitted sts by sewing them into beak with matching sewing thread.

Sew beak to penguin's face between the eyes and just below them.

Mountaineering penguin

Materials for the accessories: Oddments of double knitting yarn; a pair of 3 mm [No 11] knitting needles; two small beads for the rucksack fastening.

Make the basic penguin sewing the eyes in place 1.5 cm [$\frac{5}{8}$ in] down from the top of the head.

Rucksack

Cast on 14 sts and beginning with a K row, st-st 35 rows.

Next row: K.

Cast off.

Shoulder straps [make two alike]

Cast on 24 sts then cast off.

To make up

Fold up cast on edge of rucksack 3.5 cm [$1\frac{3}{8}$ in] having wrong side of st-st outside. Oversew side edges together. Turn right side out. Sew two loops of yarn to the cast off edge of rucksack flap, then sew two beads to rucksack to hook the two yarn loops onto.

Sew ends of shoulder straps to sides of rucksack at upper and lower edges so that they can be looped round penguin's wings.

Climbing rope

Make a tightly twisted cord from a 2 m [2 yd] length of yarn. Tie one end round penguin's waist. Sew end of one wing to the rope at waist then loop the rope round and sew it to the other wing as shown in the illustration on page 55.

Cap

Cast on 36 sts and beginning with a K row, st-st 10 rows.

Next row: (K 2 tog) to end – 18 sts.

P 1 row.

Next row: (K 2 tog) to end – 9 sts.

Break off yarn leaving a long end then thread it through remaining sts, pull up tightly and fasten off.

To make up
Oversew row ends of cap together noting that P side of cap is the right side.

For the cap bobble, wind a tiny ball of yarn leaving a long end of yarn. Thread a needle with this yarn end and take it backwards and forwards through the ball to secure all wound strands. Sew bobble to top of cap. Put the cap on penguin's head allowing the cast on edge to turn inwards. Catch cap to head.

Scarf

Cast on 54 sts and K 1 row then cast off.

Make two bobbles in same way as for the cap and sew to ends of scarf.

Penguin with skis

Materials for the accessories: Oddments of double knitting yarn; a pair of 3 mm [No 11] knitting needles; oddment of Twilley's silver Goldfingering yarn [or you can use silver gift wrapping cord as an alternative] and two flat wooden lolly sticks 1 cm by 9.5 cm [$\frac{3}{8}$ in by $3\frac{3}{4}$ in], for the skis; two 8 cm [$3\frac{1}{4}$ in] long bits of twig with forked ends for the ski poles.

Make the basic penguin sewing the eyes in place half way down the face.

Scarf

Make as for the mountaineering penguin.

Cap

Cast on 32 sts and K 1 row.

Join on another colour.

Beginning with a K row, st-st 14 rows alternating colours every 2 rows.

Keeping stripes correct shape top of cap:

Next row: (K 2 tog) to end – 16 sts.

P 1 row.

Next row: (K 2 tog) to end – 8 sts.

Break off yarn leaving a long end then thread it through remaining sts, pull up tightly and fasten off.

To make up
Join row ends of cap, back stitching the seam. Make a bobble in same way as for the scarf and sew it to top of cap then sew the cap to penguin's head. Pull top of cap over to one side and catch in place.

Skis [make two alike]

Using yarn as suggested, cast on 5 sts.

1st row: Inc K wise into every st – 10 sts.

St-st 28 rows.

Next row: (K 2 tog) to end – 5 sts.

Cast off.

To make up
Gather along the cast off sts, pull up tightly and fasten off. Oversew row ends of ski together having right side of st-st outside. Slip the lolly stick inside the knitted ski having the oversewn seam underneath ski. Gather up the cast on edge tightly and fasten off. Use same yarn as used for the skis to sew the penguin's feet to the centre of skis, taking the stitches over tops of feet.

Ski poles

Sew a twig to end of each wing as shown in the illustration.

Chef penguin with barbecue

Materials for the accessories: Oddments of double knitting yarn; a pair of 3 mm [No 11] knitting needles; oddment of Twilley's silver Goldfingering yarn [or you can use silver gift wrapping cord as an alternative] and four tiny black beads for the fish; a bit of twig with a forked end; two matchboxes, three wooden cocktail sticks and red and black marker pens for the barbecue; adhesive.

Make the basic penguin sewing the eyes in place half way down the face.

Chef's hat

Using white cast on 36 sts.

Beginning with a P row, st-st 7 rows.

Shape top of hat: *Next row:* (K 2, inc in next st) to end – 48 sts.

St-st 7 rows.

Dec for top of hat: *Next row:* (K 2, K 2 tog) to end – 36 sts.

P 1 row.

Next row: (K 1, K 2 tog) to end – 24 sts.

P 1 row.

Next row: (K 2 tog) to end – 12 sts.

Break off yarn leaving a long end then thread it through remaining sts, pull up tightly and fasten off.

To make up

Oversew row ends of hat together then sew the hat to penguin's head as shown in the illustration. Pull top of hat over to one side and catch in place.

Apron

Cast on 14 sts and st-st 10 rows then cast off.

For the waistband make a 26 cm [$10\frac{1}{2}$ in] long twisted cord from a single strand of yarn and sew cast off edge of apron to centre of waistband. Tie the apron round the penguin and catch the top and sides to the penguin.

Fish on a fork

For the fish use yarn as suggested and beginning at mouth end, cast on 2 sts.

1st row: Inc K wise into every st – 4 sts.

2nd row: P.

3rd row: Inc K wise into every st – 8 sts.

St-st 9 rows then cast off.

To make up

Having right side of st-st outside, oversew the row ends together. Push a little stuffing in fish, then wind black sewing thread tightly around the body 1 cm [$\frac{3}{8}$ in] away from the cast off edge to form the tail. To divide the tail into two fins, work black oversewing stitches tightly over the cast off edge.

Sew on the beads for the eyes and work a small black stitch for the mouth.

For the fork, use a 5 cm [2 in] length of twig with a forked portion at one end. Now glue the forked end of the stick into the fish and sew the other end of stick to the penguin's wing.

The barbecue

Take one matchbox tray, discarding the slide-on cover. Colour the inside of the tray with black pen.

To knit the coals, use grey yarn, cast on 18 sts and st-st 16 rows.

Cast off.

Colour the P side of the knitting with black pen around the edges and here and there at the centre. Mark here and there with red pen also. Now thread a needle with red yarn and work a few stitches on the knitted piece to resemble hot coals. Turn under the edges of the knitted piece and glue it inside the base of the matchbox tray.

For the barbecue grid, pierce three small holes, evenly spaced, along each short edge of the matchbox tray, close to the top edge. Push a cocktail stick through each pair of holes from one side of the tray to the other. Trim off the protruding pointed ends of the cocktail sticks, then colour sticks with black pen.

Now glue the matchbox tray on top of the other complete matchbox. To make the brick effect covering on the outside of the matchboxes, use red yarn and cast on 40 sts.

G-st 2 rows.

Beginning with a K row, st-st 11 rows then cast off.

Oversew row ends of this piece together then slip it over the matchboxes having the cast on edge level with upper edge of matchbox tray. Glue the upper and lower edges of the knitted piece in place. Mark two horizontal black lines around the barbecue, spacing them evenly, then mark vertical lines to divide into bricks as shown in the illustration.

Make a fish in the same way as made for the penguin's fish on a fork and glue it to the barbecue grid.

Fishing penguin

Materials for the accessories: Oddments of double knitting yarn; a pair of 3 mm [No 11] knitting needles; oddment of Twilley's silver Goldfingering yarn [or you can use silver gift wrapping cord as an alternative] and two tiny black beads for the fish; a 14 cm [5½ in] length of twig and thin cord for the fishing rod.

Make the basic penguin sewing the eyes in place half way down the face.

Scarf

Make as for the mountaineering penguin omitting the bobbles [see page 54].

Hat

Cast on 56 sts and g-st 3 rows.
Next row: (K 2 tog) to end – 28 sts.
Beginning with a K row, st-st 12 rows.
Next row: (K 2 tog) to end – 14 sts.
Cast off.

To make up
Join row ends of hat noting that P side of knitting is right side of hat. Join across the cast off sts.

Put the hat on the penguin's head and catch it to the head where it touches. Sew the cast off sts to penguin's head to indent the top of the hat.

Fishing rod

Tie cord to one end of the twig then make a fish in the same way as those made for the barbecue. Sew end of cord to the fish. Position the fishing rod under the end of penguin's wing as shown in the illustration and sew it to the body then sew wing to body to hold rod in place.

Penguin with snowballs

Materials for the accessories: Oddments of double knitting yarn; a pair of 3 mm [No 11] knitting needles.

Make the basic penguin sewing the eyes in place 1.5 cm [⅝ in] down from top of head.

Scarf

Make as for the mountaineering penguin.

Cap

Cast on 28 sts and K 1 row.
Beginning with a K row, st-st 6 rows.
Next row: (K 2 tog) to end – 14 sts.
P 1 row.
Next row: (K 2 tog) to end – 7 sts.
Break off yarn leaving a long end then thread it through remaining sts, pull up tightly and fasten off.

To make up
Join row ends of cap. Make a bobble in same way as for the scarf and sew it to top of cap. Sew cap to penguin's head.

Snowballs

Make four bobbles from white yarn in same way as for the scarf bobbles, then sew them to the penguin as shown in the illustration.

The snow penguin

15 cm [5¾] high

You will need: Oddment of white brushed double knitting yarn; a pair of 4 mm [No 8] knitting needles; two 6 mm [¼ in] diameter black beads; twigs for making the broom; small amount of stuffing.

To make

Work all the pieces as for the basic penguin but use two strands of yarn together, 4 mm [No 8] knitting needles and omit the chest piece.

Stuff the wings lightly and make the broom before sewing the wings in place. Sew the beads in place for the eyes as for the other penguins, half way down the face.

For the broom handle cut a 10 cm [4 in] length of twig about 5 mm [¼ in] in diameter. Cut 6 cm [2¼ in] lengths of very thin twigs and bind these around one end of the handle using strong thread. Pin the wings to each side of the penguin with the broom tucked under one wing as shown in the illustration. Sew the wings in place all round the edges where they touch the body.

Mamas and babes

A cuddlesome bunch of tiny toys which are oh-so-quick to knit. The largest, Mrs Hedgehog is just 9 cm [$3\frac{1}{2}$ in] long, while the baby bee and ladybird measure less than 5 cm [2 in].

You will need: Oddments of double knitting yarn in assorted colours, appropriate to the various creatures as shown in the illustration; a pair of $3\frac{1}{4}$ mm [No 10] knitting needles; small amount of stuffing; oddments of felt, ribbon, lace edging, and guipure flowers; adhesive.

Abbreviations: See page 17.

Mother hedgehog

9 cm [$3\frac{1}{2}$ in] long

Begin at back of hedgehog and using brown cast on 15 sts.

Next row: Inc K wise into every st – 30 sts.

Work the looped pattern: *1st row:* K 6; * insert right hand needle K wise into next st, place first finger of left hand at back of st, wind yarn anti-clockwise round needle and finger twice, then round tip of right hand needle only, draw through the 3 loops; repeat from * until 6 sts remain; K 6.

2nd row: K 6; * K 3 tog, pulling loops down firmly as you go; repeat from * until 6 sts remain; K 6 – 30 sts.

Repeat these last two rows 8 more times.

Break off brown and join on fawn for head.

Now beginning with a P row, work in st-st, decreasing 1 st at each end of every row until 12 sts remain. Break off yarn leaving a long end then thread it through remaining sts, pull up tightly and fasten off.

To make up

Oversew row ends of work together leaving cast on edge open. Turn right side out and stuff. Gather round cast on edge, pull up gathers tightly and fasten off.

Work a few stitches for nose in brown. Cut out and stick on 5 mm [$\frac{1}{4}$ in] diameter circles of black felt for the eyes.

For the hat cut a 4 cm [$1\frac{1}{2}$ in] diameter circle of felt then sew it to head through the centre of the circle. For the crown of the hat cut a 2 cm [$\frac{3}{4}$ in] diameter circle from two layers of felt glued together. Stick this to the hat then decorate it with flower trimming and a ribbon bow as shown in the illustration.

Baby hedgehog

6.5 cm [$2\frac{1}{2}$ in] long

Begin at back of hedgehog using brown and cast on 10 sts.

Next row: Inc K wise into every st – 20 sts.

Work the looped pattern: *1st row:* K 4; * insert right-hand needle K wise into next st, place first finger of left hand at back of st, wind yarn anti-clockwise round needle and finger twice, then round tip of right-hand needle only, draw through the 3 loops; repeat from * until 4 sts remain; K 4.

2nd row: K 4; * K 3 tog, pulling loops down firmly as you go; repeat from * until 4 sts remain; K 4 – 20 sts.

Repeat these two rows 5 more times.

Break off brown and join on fawn for head.

Now beginning with a P row, work in st-st decreasing 1 st at each end of every row until 8 sts remain.

Finish off and make up as for mother hedgehog, omitting the hat and making the eyes slightly smaller.

Mother mouse

8.5 cm [$3\frac{1}{4}$ in] long

Begin at back of mouse and using pink cast on 14 sts, leaving a long end of yarn for making tail later on.

Next row: Inc K wise into every st – 28 sts.

1st pattern row: K 4, P 20, K 4.

2nd pattern row: K.

Repeat these last two rows 7 more times.

Now beginning with a P row, work in st-st

decreasing 1 st at each end of every row until 12 sts remain. Break off yarn leaving a long end, thread it through remaining sts then pull up tightly and fasten off.

Ears [make two alike]

Cast on 3 sts.

1st row: Inc K wise into every st – 6 sts.

Now beginning with a P row, st-st 5 rows.

Break off yarn leaving a long end and then thread it through sts, pull up tightly and fasten off.

To make up

Gather along cast on sts of body, pull up tightly and fasten off. Twist the long end of yarn for the tail tightly, then allow it to curl up, making tail about 10 cm [4 in] in length.

Fasten off end of yarn.

Oversew row ends of work together leaving a gap for turning. Turn right side out and stuff, then oversew gap. Sew gathered edges of ears to head. Work pink stitches for the nose then cut the eyes as for mother hedgehog and stick them in place.

Gather up a bit of lace trimming tightly for the hat, sew a ribbon bow to the centre then sew hat to head.

Baby mouse

6.5 cm [$2\frac{1}{2}$ in] long

Begin at back of mouse and using pink cast on 10 sts, leaving a long end of yarn for making the tail later on.

Next row: Inc K wise into every st – 20 sts.

1st pattern row: K 3, P 14, K 3.

2nd pattern row: K.

Repeat these last two rows 5 more times.

Now beginning with a P row, work in st-st decreasing 1 st at each end of every row until 8 sts remain.

Finish off as for mother mouse.

Ears [make two alike]

Make as for mother mouse but st-st 3 rows instead of 5.

To make up

Make up as for mother mouse omitting the hat and making the eyes slightly smaller.

Make the tail in same way as mother mouse but 8 cm [3 in] in length.

Mother ladybird

6 cm [$2\frac{1}{4}$ in] long

Begin at back of ladybird and using red cast on 5 sts.

Next row: Inc K wise into every st – 10 sts.

Next row: Inc P wise into every st – 20 sts.

** *1st pattern row:* K.

2nd pattern row: K 3, P 14, K 3.

Repeat these last two rows 5 more times **.

Break off red and join on black, then repeat 1st and 2nd pattern rows 3 more times.

*** *Next row:* (K 2 tog) to end – 10 sts.

Next row: (P 2 tog) to end – 5 sts.

Break off yarn leaving a long end then thread it through remaining sts, pull up tightly and fasten off.

To make up

Gather along the cast on sts then pull up tightly and fasten off. Oversew row ends of work together leaving a gap for turning. Turn right side out and stuff, then oversew gap.

Cut 5 mm [$\frac{1}{4}$ in] diameter circles of white felt for the eyes then using a black pen, mark a small semi-circle at one side of each eye. Stick the eyes in place.

Work a long black stitch down the centre of the body then work two black spots on each side.

Gather up a bit of lace trimming and sew it around the face as shown in the illustration.

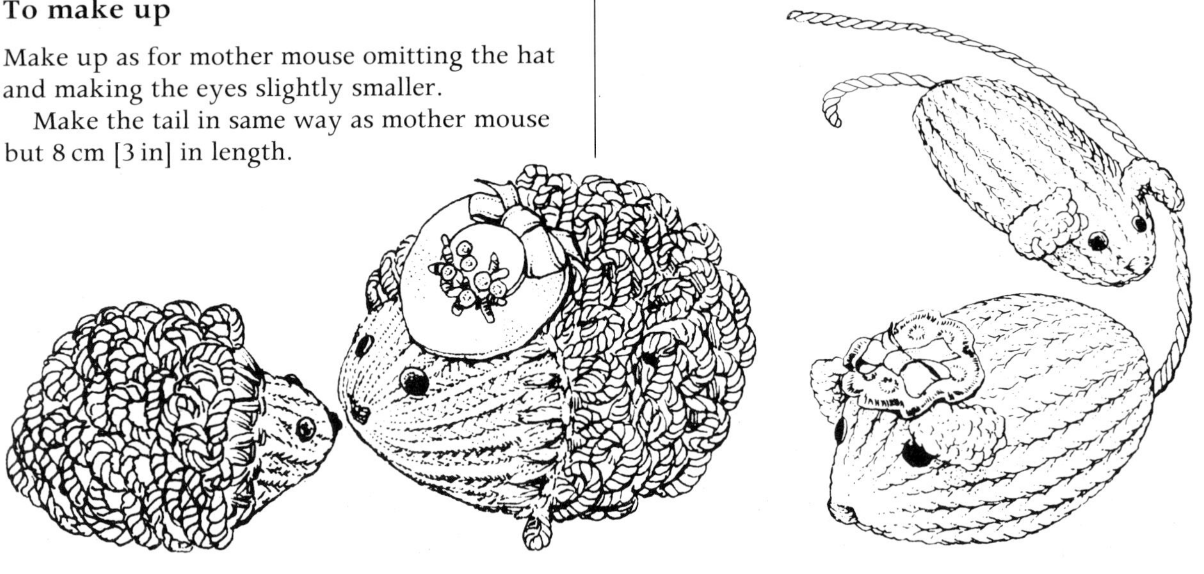

Baby ladybird

4 cm [$1\frac{1}{2}$ in] long

Begin at back of ladybird and using red cast on 4 sts.

Next row: Inc K wise into every st – 8 sts.

Next row: Inc P wise into every st – 16 sts.

** *1st pattern row:* K.

2nd pattern row: K 2, P 12, K 2.

Repeat these last two rows 3 more times **.

Break off red and join on black, then repeat 1st and 2nd pattern rows twice more.

*** *Next row:* (K 2 tog) to end – 8sts.

Next row: (P 2 tog) to end – 4 sts.

Finish off and make up as for mother ladybird, omitting the lace trim and making the eyes slightly smaller.

Mother bee

6 cm [$2\frac{1}{4}$ in] long

Begin at back of bee and using brown cast on 5 sts.

Next row: Inc K wise into every st – 10 sts.

Next row: Inc P wise into every st – 20 sts.

Join on gold and work as for mother ladybird from ** to **, working in two row stripes of gold and brown. Break off brown and continue in gold only.

St-st 6 rows.

Now work as given for mother ladybird from *** to the end.

Wings [make two alike]

Using white cast on 4 sts.

1st row: Inc K wise into every st – 8 sts.

G-st 13 rows.

Break off yarn leaving a long end, thread it through remaining sts then pull up tightly and fasten off.

To make up

Make up the body as for the ladybird. Cut eyes and stick in place as for mother hedgehog. Work a loop of black yarn above each eye and a small pink stitch for mouth.

Sew the gathered up edges of wings to the first brown stripe behind the head.

Make the hat as for mother hedgehog but use a 2 cm [$\frac{3}{4}$ in] and a 1 cm [$\frac{3}{8}$ in] diameter circle of felt.

Baby bee

4 cm [$1\frac{1}{2}$ in] long

Begin at back of bee and using brown cast on 4 sts.

Next row: Inc K wise into every st – 8 sts.

Next row: Inc P wise into every st – 16 sts.

Join on gold and work as for baby ladybird from ** to **, working in two row stripes of gold and brown. Break off brown and continue in gold only.

St-st 4 rows.

Now work as for baby ladybird from *** to end.

Wings [make two alike]

Using white cast on 3 sts.

1st row: Inc K wise into every st – 6 sts.

G-st 9 rows.

Break off yarn and finish off as for mother's wings.

To make up

Make up as for mother bee omitting the hat and making the eyes slightly smaller.

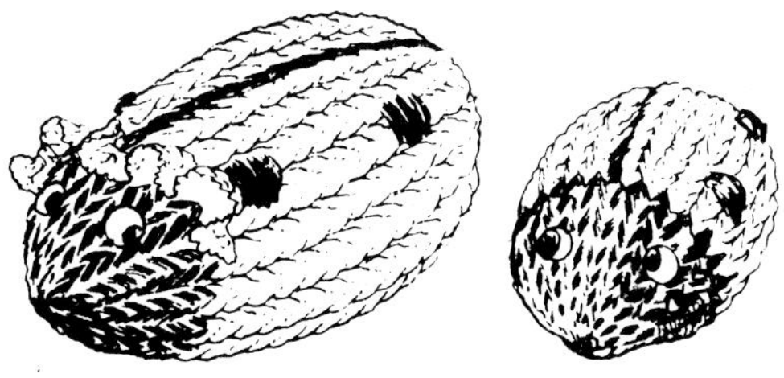

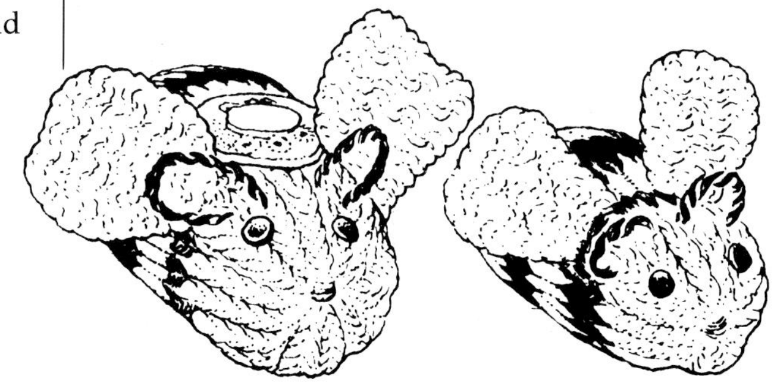

Ten of the best

Ten dolls based on one simple pattern, but with all the little extra touches that make each one an individual character.

Easy to make [the legs, body and head all knitted in one piece] and with the minimum of shaping, they are perfect for using up all your oddments of yarn. Each doll measures about 28 cm [11 in] from top to toe.

You will need: Oddments of double knitting yarn in assorted colours as shown in the illustrations; a pair of 3 mm [No 11] knitting needles; small amount of stuffing for each doll; oddments of coloured felt; lace edging, trimmings, braids and ribbons etc.; a red pencil; adhesive.

Abbreviations: See page 17.

Note: The 'main piece' for each doll includes the legs, body and head. It is knitted all in one piece beginning at the lower [ankle] edge and ending at the top of the head. The legs are formed at the making up stage by sewing through the centre of the body from front to back.

Robin Hood

The main piece

Begin at ankle edge and using dark green cast on 40 sts.

Now starting with a K row, work in st-st throughout breaking off and joining on colours as required.

Work 26 rows in dark green.
6 rows in light green.
4 rows in tan.
14 rows in light green.

Continuing in light green, dec for shoulders: *Next row:* K 6, K 2 tog, K 4, K 2 tog, K 12, K 2 tog, K 4, K 2 tog, K 6 – 36 sts.

Now work 3 rows in light green.
2 rows in pink.

Continuing in pink, inc for head:
Next row: K 6, inc in next st, K 4, inc in next st, K 12, inc in next st, K 4, inc in next st, K 6 – 40 sts.

Work 25 rows in pink.

Next row: (K 2 tog) to end – 20 sts.

Break off yarn leaving a long end then thread it loosely through remaining sts and leave.

The arms [make two alike]

Begin at top of arm and using light green cast on 16 sts.

St-st 26 rows then change to pink.
St-st 8 rows.
Next row: (K 2 tog) to end – 8 sts.

Break off yarn leaving a long end. Thread it through remaining sts then pull up tightly and fasten off.

The shoes [make two alike]

Using brown cast on 10 sts and st-st 6 rows.
Inc 1 st at each end of the next row – 12 sts.
St-st 5 rows.
Inc 1 st at each end of the next row – 14 sts.
St-st 13 rows.
Dec 1 st at each end of the next row – 12 sts.
St-st 5 rows.
Dec 1 st at each end of the next row – 10 sts.
St-st 5 rows then cast off.

The cap

Begin at lower edge and using dark green cast on 50 sts and st-st 7 rows.

Change to light green and beginning with a K row, st-st 14 rows.

Cast off.

Note that the K side of the light green portion will be right side of the cap when making up.

To make up

Main piece
At the cast on edge of the main piece, mark

position of the exact centre of the row with a coloured thread. Join row ends of the main piece [this seam will be at centre back of the doll] then turn right side out.

Now catch the marked centre front point of cast on edge to the centre back seam. Continue sewing back and forth through the doll at the centre position for 7 cm [$2\frac{3}{4}$ in] up the body, to form the legs.

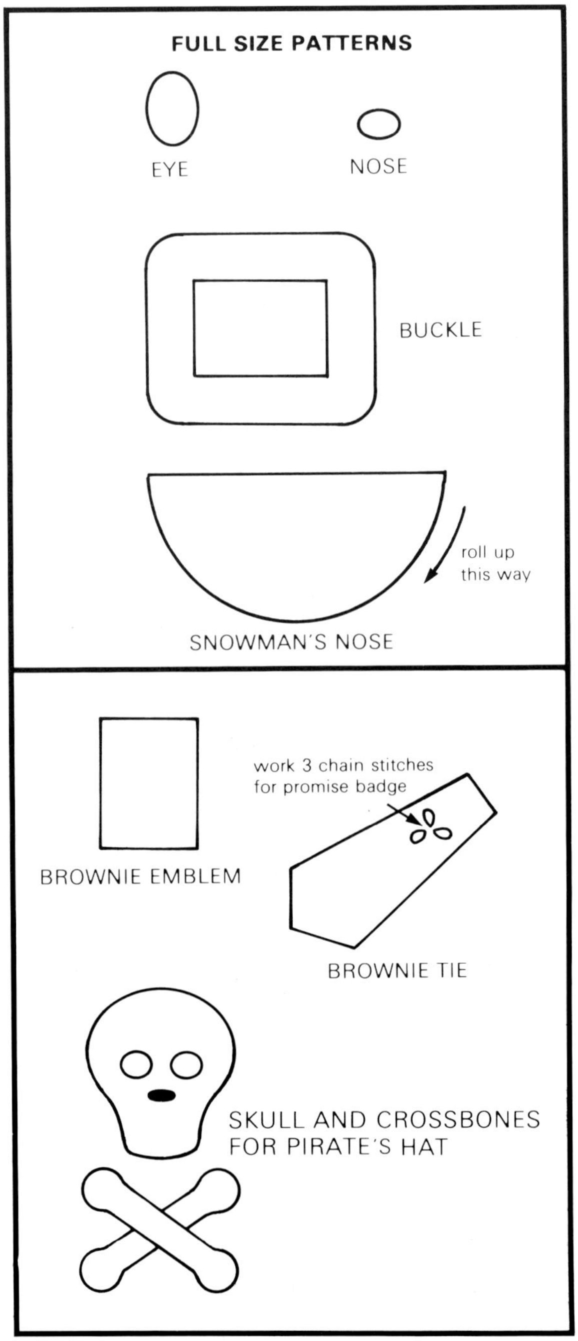

Stuff the body and head through the opening at top of head, then stuff the legs through the lower edges. Pull up length of yarn tightly at top of head and fasten off.

To shape the neck, tie a length of matching yarn tightly round at lower edge of head then sew ends of yarn into body.

Face
Work two stitches in red for the mouth forming a V-shape, 2.5 cm [1 in] up from the neck. Cut the eyes from black felt and the nose from red felt using the patterns then glue them in place. Colour the cheeks with red pencil.

Arms
Join the row ends of each arm leaving the cast on edges open. Turn right side out and stuff. Oversew the top edges of each arm together, then sew tops of arms to each side of the body 1.5 cm [$\frac{5}{8}$ in] down from the neck.

Shoes
Bring the cast on and cast off edges of each shoe together and join the edges, rounding off the corners and leaving a gap for turning. Turn right side out and stuff firmly then ladder stitch the gap. Place a shoe under the open end of each leg, having shoes at right angles to legs. Slip stitch ankle edges of legs to the shoes.

Hair
Using a suitable colour for the hair wind yarn round and round a 2 cm by 20 cm [$\frac{3}{4}$ in by 8 in] strip of thick paper to cover it. Machine stitch through the loops close to one long edge, then tear the paper away. If you do not have a sewing machine then back stitch the loops together along one edge of the paper. Sew this looped fringe round the doll's head.

Cap
Fold cap in half, bringing the row ends together. Sew across the cast off edge and round off the corner before joining the row ends. Turn cap right side out and sew lower edge to head, lapping it over top edge of hair.

Sew a small feather to one side of the cap if desired.

Finishing touches
Cut the buckle from felt using the pattern then

stick it in place. Sew ric-rac braid round the neck-line, the wrist edges and the lower edge of the light green on the body, as shown in the illustration.

The footballer

The main piece

Begin at ankle edge and using blue cast on 40 sts.

Now starting with a K row, work in st-st throughout breaking off and joining colours as required.

Work 8 rows in blue.
2 rows in white.
2 rows in blue.
22 rows in pink.
16 rows in blue.

Continuing in blue, dec for shoulders: *Next row:* K 6, K 2 tog, K 4, K 2 tog, K 12, K 2 tog, K 4, K 2 tog, K 6 – 36 sts.

Now work 3 rows in white.
2 rows in pink.

Continuing in pink, inc for head: *Next row:* K 6, inc in next st, K 4, inc in next st, K 12, inc in next st, K 4, inc in next st, K 6 – 40 sts.

Work 25 rows in pink.

Next row: (K 2 tog) to end – 20 sts.

Break off yarn leaving a long end then thread it loosely through remaining sts and leave.

The arms [make two alike]

Begin at top of arm and using blue cast on 16 sts.

St-st 24 rows then change to white.

St-st 2 rows then change to pink.

St-st 8 rows.

Next row: (K 2 tog) to end – 8 sts.

Break off yarn leaving a long end. Thread it through remaining sts then pull up tightly and fasten off.

The shoes [make two alike]

Using black make exactly as for Robin Hood [see page 63].

The shorts

Using white cast on 50 sts and K 1 row.

Beginning with a K row, st-st 13 rows.

Dec for waist: *Next row:* (P 3, P 2 tog) to end – 40 sts. Cast off.

To make up

Make up the main piece, arms and shoes, and add facial features as for Robin Hood [see pages 63 and 64].

Hair
Make loops for the hair in the same way as for Robin Hood, then continue adding rows of yarn loops above the first row, to cover the top of the head.

Shorts
Join the row ends of the shorts. Turn right side out then place them on the doll having seam at centre back. Sew the cast off edge to the first row of blue on the body. Catch centre front of the shorts at cast on edge, to centre back seam taking stitches right through doll at centre.

The snowman

The main piece

Begin at ankle edge and using white cast on 40 sts.

Now starting with a K row, st-st 50 rows.

Dec for shoulders: *Next row:* K 6, K 2 tog, K 4, K 2 tog, K 12, K 2 tog, K 4, K 2 tog, K 6 – 36 sts.

St-st 5 rows.

Inc for head: *Next row:* K 6, inc in next st, K 4, inc in next st, K 12, inc in next st, K 4, inc in next st, K 6 – 40 sts.

St-st 25 rows.

Next row: (K 2 tog) to end – 20 sts.

Break off yarn leaving a long end. Thread it loosely through remaining sts and leave.

The arms [make two alike]

Begin at top of arm and using white cast on 16 sts.

St-st 34 rows.
Next row: (K 2 tog) to end – 8 sts.
Break off yarn leaving a long end. Thread it through remaining sts then pull up tightly and fasten off.

The shoes [make two alike]

Using white, make exactly as for Robin Hood [see page 63].

The scarf

Using red cast on 6 sts and work in g-st until scarf measures 34 cm [$13\frac{1}{2}$ in]. Add fringe tassles in yellow to each end of scarf.

The hat

Using green cast on 50 sts and beginning with a K row, st-st 7 rows.
Now beginning with a K row, st-st 20 rows working in two row stripes of the colours of your choice.
Keeping sequence of stripes correct shape the top: * *Next row:* (K 3, K 2 tog) to end – 40 sts.
P 1 row.
Next row: (K 2, K 2 tog) to end – 30 sts.
P 1 row.
Next row: (K 1, K 2 tog) to end – 20 sts.
P 1 row.
Next row: (K 2 tog) to end – 10 sts.
Break off yarn leaving a long end. Thread it through remaining sts then pull up tightly and fasten off. Note that the K side of the upper portion of the hat will be right side when making up.

To make up

Make up the main piece, arms and shoes as for Robin Hood [see pages 63 and 64].

Face
Add mouth and eyes as for Robin Hood using black for the mouth stitch. Cut the nose from orange felt using the pattern on page 64. Roll it up to make a carrot shape sewing the edge in place, then sew nose to face.

Hat
Join row ends of hat. Turn right side out and sew lower edge to head. Pull top of hat over to one side as shown in the illustration then catch in place at this position. Make a small pom-pon and sew it to top of hat.

Finishing touches
Tie the scarf round snowman's neck. Sew three small irregular circles of black felt down the front of the body.

Santa Claus

The main piece

Begin at ankle edge and using black cast on 40 sts.
Now starting with a K row, work in st-st except where instructions say to work in g-st; breaking off and joining on colours as required.
Work 8 rows in black.
4 rows g-st in white.
12 rows in red.
4 rows g-st in white.
4 rows in red.
4 rows in green.
14 rows in red.
Continuing in red dec for shoulders:
Next row: K 6, K 2 tog, K 4, K 2 tog, K 12, K 2 tog, K 4, K 2 tog, K 6 – 36 sts.
Now work 3 rows in red.
2 rows in pink.
Continuing in pink, inc for head:
Next row: K 6, inc in next st, K 4, inc in next st, K 12, inc in next st, K 4, inc in next st, K 6 – 40 sts.
Work 25 rows in pink.
Next row: (K 2 tog) to end – 20 sts.
Break off yarn leaving a long end. Thread it loosely through remaining sts and leave.

The arms [make two alike]

Begin at top of arm and using red cast on 16 sts.
St-st 22 rows then change to white.
G-st 4 rows then change to pink.
St-st 8 rows.

Next row: (K 2 tog) to end – 8 sts.
Break off yarn leaving a long end. Thread it

through remaining sts then pull up tightly and fasten off.

The shoes [make two alike]

Using black, make exactly as for Robin Hood [see page 63].

The hat

Using white cast on 50 sts and beginning with a K row, st-st 7 rows. Change to red and beginning with a K row, st-st 20 rows.

Now work as given for the snowman's hat from * to the end [see page opposite].

The beard

Using brushed white yarn [or you can use plain yarn and brush the beard after knitting], cast on 30 sts.

Work in g-st, decreasing 1 st at each end of next and every following alternate row until 2 sts remain.

K the 2 remaining sts together then fasten off.

To make up

Make up the main piece, arms and shoes and add facial features as for Robin Hood [see pages 63 and 64].

Beard
Sew beard below mouth as illustrated.

Hat
Join row ends of hat. Turn right side out and put it on Santa's head to cover sides of beard. Sew lower edge of hat to head enclosing a few loops of white yarn above eyes for the hair.

Make a small red pom-pon and sew to top of hat.

Finishing touches
Cut the buckle from felt using the pattern then stick it in place.

Cinderella

The main piece

Begin at ankle edge and using pink cast on 40 sts.

Now starting with a K row, work in st-st throughout breaking off and joining on colours as required.

Work 26 rows in pink.
12 rows in white.
12 rows in yellow.

Continuing in yellow, dec for shoulders:

Next row: K 6, K 2 tog, K 4, K 2 tog, K 12, K 2 tog, K 4, K 2 tog, K 6 – 36 sts.

Now work 3 rows in yellow.
2 rows in pink.

Continuing in pink, inc for head:

Next row: K 6, inc in next st, K 4, inc in next st, K 12, inc in next st, K 4, inc in next st, K 6 – 40 sts.

Work 25 rows in pink.

Next row: (K 2 tog) to end – 20 sts.

Break off yarn leaving a long end. Thread it loosely through remaining sts and leave.

The arms [make two alike]

Begin at top of arm and using yellow cast on 16 sts.

St-st 26 rows then change to pink and st-st 8 rows.

Next row: (K 2 tog) to end – 8 sts.

Break off yarn leaving a long end. Thread it through remaining sts then pull up tightly and fasten off.

The shoes [make two alike]

Using dark blue, make exactly as for Robin Hood [see page 63].

Apron

Skirt

Using lilac cast on 60 sts and K 1 row.

Beginning with a K row, st-st 32 rows.

Dec for waist: *Next row:* (K 1, K 2 tog) to end – 40 sts.

Cast off.

Bib

Using lilac cast on 12 sts.

K 1 row, then beginning with a K row, st-st 10 rows.

Cast off.

Patches

Make these in assorted colours. Cast on 6 sts and st-st 6 rows then cast off.

Cap

Using white cast on 100 sts.

G-st 4 rows.

Next row: (K 2 tog) to end – 50 sts.

Beginning with a K row, st-st 20 rows.

Now work as given for the snowman's hat from * to the end [see page 66].

To make up

Make up the main piece, arms and shoes and add facial features as for Robin Hood [see pages 63 and 64].

Hair

Cut twenty-four 30 cm [12 in] lengths of yarn in a suitable colour for hair. Tie them together at centre with a strand of matching yarn. Sew the centre to the doll's forehead then sew the strands to each side of head, level with the mouth. Plait the strands and tie ribbon bows round the ends.

Cap

Join the row ends of the cap and turn it right side out. Stuff the top to make a nice rounded shape. Put the cap on doll's head behind the hair then sew it in place through the decrease row. Sew a ribbon bow to front of cap.

Apron

Join row ends of skirt and turn right side out. Sew the knitted patches to skirt using contrasting yarn. Pin the cast off edge of skirt level with the first row of yellow on the body, having the seam at centre back. Tuck cast off edge of bib inside the skirt at centre front. Pin the ends of two lengths of ribbon inside top of bib at front, take ribbons over shoulders and cross them over at back then tuck other ends inside waist edge of skirt. Sew the waist edge of skirt to doll. Sew bib to doll catching in the ends of the ribbon.

Finishing touches

Sew ric-rac braid round the wrists.

Davy Crockett

The main piece

Begin at ankle edge and using fawn cast on 40 sts.

Now starting with a K row, work in st-st throughout breaking off and joining on colours as required.

Work 32 rows in fawn.
4 rows in brown.
14 rows in fawn.

Continuing in fawn, dec for shoulders:

Next row: K 6, K 2 tog, K 4, K 2 tog, K 12, K 2 tog, K 4, K 2 tog, K 6 – 36 sts.

Now work 3 rows in fawn.
2 rows in pink.

Continuing in pink, inc for head:

Next row: K 6, inc in next st, K 4, inc in next st, K 12, inc in next st, K 4, inc in next st, K 6 – 40 sts.

Work 25 rows in pink.

Next row: (K 2 tog) to end – 20 sts.
Break off yarn leaving a long end. Thread it loosely through remaining sts and leave.

The arms [make two alike]

Begin at top of arm and using fawn cast on 16 sts.
St-st 26 rows then change to pink and st-st 8 rows.
Next row: (K 2 tog) to end – 8 sts.
Break off yarn leaving a long end. Thread it through remaining sts then pull up tightly and fasten off.

The shoes [make two alike]

Using brown, make exactly as for Robin Hood [see page 63].

Cap

Using brushed brown yarn [or you can use plain yarn and brush the cap after knitting], cast on 50 sts.
St-st 26 rows.
Now work as given for the snowman's hat from * to the end [see page 66].
For the raccoon tail use brown yarn and cast on 12 sts.
St-st 12 rows, working in two row stripes of brown and dark brown.
Keeping sequence of stripes correct, dec 1 st at each end of every K row until 2 sts remain.
Break off yarn and fasten off the 2 remaining sts.

To make up

Make up the main piece, arms and shoes and add facial features as for Robin Hood [see pages 63 and 64].

Hair
Add hair in the same way as for Robin Hood [see page 64].

Cap
Join row ends of cap then turn right side out. Turn in 3 cm [$1\frac{1}{4}$ in] at lower edge of cap. Sew cap to head just lapping it over the hair loops.
Join row ends of raccoon tail and turn right side out then sew cast on edge to lower edge of cap at one side.

Finishing touches
For the fringes use fawn yarn and a bodkin to loop strands of yarn through the body, three knitted rows below the brown stripe. Trim ends of yarn evenly.
Add fringe in the same way down the outside of each arm. Work cross stitches up centre front of upper body and tie yarn strands in a bow at top as shown in the illustration.
Cut the buckle from felt using the pattern and glue it in place.

Red Riding Hood

The main piece
Begin at ankle edge and using white cast on 40 sts.
Now starting with a K row, work in st-st throughout breaking off and joining on colours as required.
Work 38 rows in white.
12 rows in turquoise.
Continuing in turquoise, dec for shoulders: *Next row:* K 6, K 2 tog, K 4, K 2 tog, K 12, K 2 tog, K 4, K 2 tog, K 6 – 36 sts.
Now work 3 rows in turquoise.
2 rows in pink.
Continuing in pink, inc for head:
Next row: K 6, inc in next st, K 4, inc in next st, K 12, inc in next st, K 4, inc in next st, K 6 – 40 sts.
Work 25 rows in pink.
Next row: (K 2 tog) to end – 20 sts.
Break off yarn leaving a long end. Thread it loosely through remaining sts and leave.

The arms [make two alike]

Begin at top of arm and using turquoise cast on 16 sts.
St-st 26 rows then change to pink and st-st 8 rows.
Next row: (K 2 tog) to end – 8 sts.
Break off yarn leaving a long end. Thread it through remaining sts then pull up tightly and fasten off.

The shoes [make two alike]

Using red, make exactly as for Robin Hood [see page 63].

Hood

Using red throughout, work in exactly the same way as given for the snowman's hat [see page 66].

Cape

Using red cast on 50 sts and K 1 row.
Beginning with a K row, st-st 13 rows.
Dec for neck: *Next row:* (P 3, P 2 tog) to end – 40 sts.
Cast off.

Skirt

Using turquoise cast on 60 sts and K 1 row.
Beginning with a K row, st-st 20 rows.
Dec for waist: *Next row:* (K 1, K 2 tog) to end – 40 sts.
Cast off.

To make up

Make up the main piece, arms and shoes and add facial features as for Robin Hood [see pages 63 to 64].

Hair
Add hair as for Cinderella [see page 68], but instead of plaiting the yarn strands, take them to centre back of head and sew there.

Hood and cape
Join the row ends of the hood for 3 cm [$1\frac{1}{4}$ in] only, leaving remainder open to sew to the cast off edge of the cape. Sew hood to cape. Sew lengths of ribbon to each side of hood to tie in a bow under the chin as shown in the illustration.

Skirt
Join row ends of skirt and turn right side out. Sew ric-rac braid around lower edge. Put skirt on doll having seam at centre back, then sew cast off edge to the first row of turquoise on the body.

Finishing touches
Sew lace trimming round the ankles and a length of fancy braid round the waist. Add ric-rac round the wrists to match the skirt trimming.

The brownie

For the brownie, it is necessary to make the skirt first so that it can be knitted into the main piece later on.

Skirt

Using tan cast on 50 sts and K 1 row.
Beginning with a K row, st-st 13 rows.
Dec for waist: *Next row:* (P 3, P 2 tog) to end – 40 sts.
Leave sts on a spare needle.

The main piece

Begin at ankle edge and using fawn cast on 40 sts.
Now starting with a K row, work in st-st throughout breaking off and joining on colours as required.
Work 6 rows in fawn.
20 rows in pink.
8 rows in dark brown.
Join on the skirt piece: Continuing in dark brown, insert right hand needle into first skirt st on the spare needle and also into first st of the main piece, K the 2 sts tog. Repeat this to the end of the row – 40 sts.
Now work 3 rows in dark brown.
12 rows in tan.
Continuing in tan, dec for shoulders:
Next row: K 6, K 2 tog, K 4, K 2 tog, K 12, K 2 tog, K 4, K 2 tog, K 6 – 36 sts.
Now work 3 rows in tan.
2 rows in pink.
Continuing in pink, inc for head:
Next row: K 6, inc in next st, K 4, inc in next st, K 12, inc in next st, K 4, inc in next st, K 6 – 40 sts.
Work 25 rows in pink.
Next row: (K 2 tog) to end – 20 sts.
Break off yarn leaving a long end. Thread it loosely through remaining sts and leave.

The arms [make two alike]

Begin at top of arm and using tan cast on 16 sts.

St-st 26 rows then change to pink and st-st 8 rows.

Next row: (K 2 tog) to end – 8 sts.

Break off yarn leaving a long end. Thread it through remaining sts then pull up tightly and fasten off.

The shoes [make two alike]

Using dark brown, make exactly as for Robin Hood [see page 63].

The pockets [make two alike]

Using tan cast on 7 sts.

Beginning with a P row st-st 6 rows then cast off.

The collar

Using tan cast on 30 sts and st-st 4 rows.
Break off yarn leaving a long end then thread it loosely through the sts and leave.

The cap

Using dark brown cast on 50 sts and beginning with a K row, st-st 7 rows.
Now beginning with a K row, st-st 20 more rows.
Work as given for the snowman's hat from * to the end [see page 66).

To make up

Make up the main piece, arms and shoes and add facial features as for Robin Hood [see pages 63 and 64].

Hair
Add hair as for Cinderella [see page 68], but trim the yarn strands shorter instead of plaiting.

Cap
Join row ends of the cap and turn right side out. Turn up the first 7 rows and catch the cast on edge to the cap. Sew the cap to head just behind the hair. Make a small pom-pon and sew it to top of cap.

Pockets
Sew the pockets to the front of the skirt as shown in the illustration.

Collar
Place the collar round the neck then pull up the strand of yarn tightly and catch ends of collar together at neck edge.

Finishing touches
Cut two tie pieces from yellow felt using the pattern on page 64. Work three small white chain stitches on one tie piece for the promise badge. Sew the tie pieces in place just under the collar crossing them over as shown in the illustration.
Cut the emblem badge from brown felt and embroider the appropriate figure on it. Sew badge in place on the doll as shown in the illustration.

Work a buckle on the belt at front using white yarn.

The guardsman

The main piece

Begin at ankle edge and using black cast on 40 sts.
Now starting with a K row, work in st-st throughout breaking off and joining on colours as required.
Work 26 rows in black.
6 rows in red.
4 rows in white.
14 rows in red.
Continuing in red, dec for shoulders:
Next row: K 6, K 2 tog, K 4, K 2 tog, K 12, K 2 tog, K 4, K 2 tog, K 6 – 36 sts.
Now work 3 rows in red.
2 rows in pink.
Continuing in pink, inc for head:
Next row: K 6, inc in next st, K 4, inc in next st, K 12, inc in next st, K 4, inc in next st, K 6 – 40 sts.
Work 25 rows in pink
Next row: (K 2 tog) to end – 20 sts.
Break off yarn leaving a long end. Thread it loosely through remaining sts and leave.

The arms [make two alike]

Begin at top of arm and using red cast on 16 sts.
St-st 22 rows then change to black.
St-st 4 rows then change to pink and st-st 8 rows.
Next row: (K 2 tog) to end – 8 sts.
Break off yarn leaving a long end. Thread it through remaining sts then pull up tightly and fasten off.

The shoes [make two alike]

Using black, make exactly as for Robin Hood [see page 63].

The hat

Using black cast on 50 sts and st-st 26 rows.

Now work as given for the snowman's hat from * to the end [see page 66].

To make up

Make up the main piece, arms and shoes and add facial features as for Robin Hood [see pages 63 and 64].

Hat
Join row ends of hat noting that P side of work will be right side of hat. Sew a length of braid under the guardsman's chin taking it up the sides of the head. Stuff top of hat then sew the cast on edge to the head as shown in the illustration, adding more stuffing if necessary to make a nice rounded shape.

The finishing touches
Use gold yarn to work a row of small stitches for buttons down the centre front of tunic. Work stitches for a belt buckle.

The pirate

The main piece

Begin at ankle edge and using dark blue cast on 40 sts.

Now starting with a K row, work in st-st throughout breaking off and joining on colours as required.

Work 32 rows in dark blue.
4 rows in black.
14 rows in two row stripes of red and gold, alternately.

Keeping sequence of stripes correct, dec for shoulders: *Next row:* K 6, K 2 tog, K 4, K 2 tog, K 12, K 2 tog, K 4, K 2 tog, K 6 – 36 sts.

Now work 3 rows, keeping sequence of stripes correct. Work 2 rows in pink.

Continuing in pink, inc for head:
Next row: K 6, inc in next st, K 4, inc in next st, K 12, inc in next st, K 4, inc in next st, K 6 – 40 sts.

Work 25 rows in pink
Next row: (K 2 tog) to end – 20 sts.

Break off yarn leaving a long end. Thread it loosely through remaining sts and leave.

Arms [make two alike]

Begin at top of arm and using red cast on 16 sts.

St-st 26 rows working in two row stripes of red and gold alternately, to match those on the body.

Change to pink and st-st 8 rows.
Next row: (K 2 tog) to end – 8 sts.

Break off yarn leaving a long end. Thread it through remaining sts then pull up tightly and fasten off.

The shoes [make two alike]

Using dark brown, make exactly as for Robin Hood [see page 63].

The hat [make two pieces alike]

Using black cast on 40 sts and st-st 6 rows.

Cast off 4 sts at beginning of next 4 rows – 24 sts.

Now dec 1 st at each end of next and every following row until 16 sts remain.
Next row: (K 2 tog) to end – 8 sts. Cast off.

To make up

Make up the main piece, arms and shoes and add facial features as for Robin Hood [see pages 63 and 64].

Hair
Make as for Robin Hood (see page 64).

Hat
Join the hat pieces at the row ends and across the cast off edges. Join the cast on edges for 2.5 cm [1 in] only at each side. Turn the hat right side out and stuff the side pieces, also put a little stuffing in top. Sew the lower edge of hat to head to cover top loops of the hair.

The finishing touches
Sew narrow braid round the lower edge of the hat. Cut the skull and crossbones pieces from white felt using the patterns on page 64. Mark the eyes and nose on the skull with black pen then glue the pieces to the hat as shown in the illustration.

Cut the buckle from felt using the pattern and stick it in place.

Topsy-turvy dolly

A novelty doll which can be transformed from sleeping to waking in an instant, simply by reversing the skirt. She measures 37 cm [$14\frac{1}{2}$ in] from the top of the head to lower edge of the skirt.

You will need: Two 20 g balls of pale pink double knitting yarn for the heads and arms; three 20 g balls of deep pink double knitting yarn for the sleepy-faced doll's nightdress; four 20 g balls of turquoise double knitting yarn for the wide-awake doll's day dress; one 20 g ball of brown 4 ply yarn for the hair; oddments of double knitting yarn in white, red and purple for trimming the dresses; short lengths of deep pink and black yarn for the facial features; a pair of 3 mm [No 11] knitting needles; small amount of stuffing; scrap of dark blue felt for the eyes; short length of tape or bias binding; a red pencil.

Abbreviations: See page 17.

The body and head

Begin at waist edge of one body and using deep pink cast on 48 sts.

Beginning with a K row, st-st 14 rows.

Shape shoulders: *Next row:* K 10, (K 2 tog) twice, K 20, (K 2 tog) twice, K 10 – 44 sts.

St-st 5 rows then break off deep pink and join on pale pink.

St-st 2 rows.

Inc for head: *Next row:* K 10, inc in next 2 sts, K 20, inc in next 2 sts, K 10 – 48 sts.

St-st 27 rows.

Next row: (K 1, K 2 tog) to end – 32 sts.

Next row: P.

Next row: (K 2 tog) to end – 16 sts.

Break off yarn leaving a long end and thread it loosely through remaining sts.

Make another piece in the same way using turquoise for the body instead of deep pink.

Nightdress arms with short sleeves [make two alike]

Begin at top of arm and using deep pink cast on 16 sts.

1st row: Inc K wise into every st – 32 sts.

Now beginning with a P row, st-st 11 rows.

Next row: (K 2 tog) to end – 16 sts.

Break off deep pink and join on purple.

G-st 5 rows. Break off purple and join on pale pink then beginning with a K row, st-st 22 rows.

Next row: (K 2 tog) to end – 8 sts. Break off yarn leaving a long end then thread it through remaining sts, pull up tightly and fasten off.

Day dress arms with long sleeves [make two alike]

Begin at top of arm and using turquoise cast on 16 sts.

1st row: Inc K wise into every st – 32 sts.

Now beginning with a P row, st-st 23 rows.

Next row: (K 2 tog) to end – 16 sts. Break off turquoise and join on red then g-st 5 rows.

Break off red and join on pale pink.

Beginning with a K row, st-st 10 rows.

Next row: (K 2 tog) to end – 8 sts. Break off yarn leaving a long end then thread it through remaining sts, pull up tightly and fasten off.

The skirts [make two alike, one in deep pink and one in turquoise]

Using white for the lacy edging, begin at lower edge and cast on 145 sts.

1st row: (K 1, take yarn once round tip of right hand needle, K 2 tog) to last st, K 1.

2nd row: K.

3rd row: K 1, (K 1, take yarn once round tip of right hand needle, K 2 tog) to end.

4th row: K.

Repeat 1st row once more. *

G-st next 3 rows. Break off white and join on purple or red, then g-st 4 rows.

Break off purple or red and join on deep pink or turquoise.

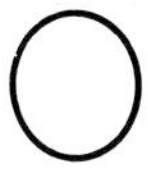

EYE

FULL SIZE PATTERN

Next 2 rows: P.

Now beginning with a K row, continue in st-st until work measures 22 cm [$8\frac{3}{4}$ in] from cast on edge, ending with a P row.

Shape for waist: *Next row:* K 1, (K 1, K 2 tog) to end – 97 sts.

Next row: P.

Next row: K 1, (K 2 tog) to end – 49 sts. Cast off knitwise.

Lace collar [make two alike]

Using white cast on 73 sts.

Work as given for skirt as far as *.

Next row: K.

Next row: (K 1, K 2 tog) to last st, K 1 – 49 sts. Cast off.

To make up the doll

Join the body pieces at cast on edges oversewing them neatly together. Now join row ends of both bodies and heads, leaving tops of heads open. Turn right side out and stuff, then draw up sts at top of each head and fasten off. Tie a strand of pink yarn tightly round each neck to shape it, then sew ends of yarn into necks.

For nose use deep pink yarn and work a small straight stitch across centre of each face 4 cm [$1\frac{1}{2}$ in] up from neck. For the mouth on the sleeping face, work a straight stitch in pink a bit longer than the nose, 2 cm [$\frac{3}{4}$ in] below nose, then work a small vertical stitch st centre of mouth. For mouth on the wide-awake face, work a V-shape below nose.

Cut wide-awake eyes from felt using the pattern then sew them to the face on either side of nose, placing them about 2 cm [$\frac{3}{4}$ in] apart. For the sleeping eyes, work small shallow V-shapes in black yarn about 2 cm [$\frac{3}{4}$ in] apart on either side of nose. Colour cheeks with red pencil.

The hair [the same for each head]

Wind the ball of 4 ply into a hank measuring about 36 cm [$14\frac{1}{2}$ in] across. Cut through the hank at each looped end, to form two groups of 36 cm [$14\frac{1}{2}$ in] lengths of yarn. For a fringe, sew a few loops of yarn to each forehead about 5 cm [2 in] above the nose. Cut a 14 cm [$5\frac{1}{2}$ in] length of tape for each head and machine stitch or back stitch centres of yarn lengths to each tape leaving 1 cm [$\frac{3}{8}$ in] of tape uncovered at each end. Turn under these ends of the tape and pin one end to each forehead above fringe and other end to head at back above neck. Sew to heads through stitching lines on tapes. Gather strands of yarn to sides of each head and sew there in bunches. Trim ends of yarn to even lengths.

The arms

Join row ends of each arm. Turn right side out and stuff, filling tops of arms quite lightly. Oversew top edges of each arm together having arm seam at centre back. Sew top edges to sides of body 1 cm [$\frac{3}{8}$ in] down from neck.

The skirts

On each skirt work the flowers as shown in the illustrations round the lower edge as follows. Use purple or red yarn to work four lazy daisy stitches for each flower, spacing the flowers about 4 cm [$1\frac{1}{2}$ in] apart, measuring between centres of flowers. Work two stitches in white at centre of each one.

Now join skirts to each other at cast on edges, oversewing edges neatly together. Join row ends of both skirts. Turn skirts right side out and bring the cast off waist edges together. Put the skirts on the doll having the seams at centre back of the doll. Pin, then sew the waist edge of one skirt just above the centre body seam. Attach second skirt in same way.

Place one collar round one neck and oversew ends together at centre back of doll. Sew cast off edge of collar to back of neck then to front of body as illustrated, to form a square neckline. Sew cast on edge of collar to front and back of body but leave collar free where it passes over each arm. Repeat with the other collar.

For each belt, make a twisted cord from a 2.5 m [$2\frac{3}{4}$ yd] length of purple or red yarn. Knot ends of cord and trim close to knots. Tie a belt round each waist making a bow at centre back. Make a short twisted cord from a single strand of purple or red yarn, tie in a bow and sew to neck edge of dress or nightdress at front.

Christmas tree trims

Here is a colourful collection of Christmas decorations which take no time at all to make. Knit some for the tree or make the little figures for the children as last minute stocking fillers. The bauble measures 5 cm [2 in] in diameter and each little figure is 9 cm [3½ in] high from top to toe.

You will need: Oddments of double knitting yarn in assorted colours as shown in the illustration; a pair of 3¼ mm [No 10] knitting needles; small amount of stuffing; scraps of narrow lurex braid; pipe cleaners for the candy canes; a red pencil; adhesive.

Abbreviations: See page 17.

To make the bauble

Begin at the lower edge of the bauble and with colour of your choice cast on 13 sts.

1st row: Inc K wise into every st – 26 sts.

St-st 16 rows.

Next row: (K 2 tog) to end – 13 sts. Break off yarn leaving a long end then thread it loosely through remaining sts. Gather the cast on edge up tightly and fasten off then join row ends of bauble. Turn right side out and stuff firmly. Make a twisted cord from a single strand of yarn making cord about 14 cm [5½ in] in length. Knot ends together and push knot inside top of bauble. Pull up length of yarn tightly at top of bauble and fasten off, oversewing to hold the cord in place. Glue a strip of braid round the centre of the bauble.

To make the candy cane

Using white cast on 12 sts. St-st 40 rows. Break off yarn leaving a long end then thread it through sts. Pull up tightly and fasten off. Bend round 1 cm [⅜ in] at each end of a pipe cleaner. Place the pipe cleaner along the length of the knitted piece then roll it up across the width and sew the long edge in place. Sew across the ends then bend into the walking stick shape.

Thread a needle with double red yarn and secure ends of yarn at one end of the candy cane. Wind yarn round and round cane as illustrated then secure at the other end. Make a twisted cord as for the bauble. Push the knotted end of the cord between the knitted stitches at the top of the cane, then oversew the stitches with sewing thread to hold the knot in place.

To make the Christmas stocking

Begin at top of stocking and with colour of your choice cast on 20 sts and K 1 row. Beginning with a K row st-st 16 rows.

Shape heel as follows: *1st row:* K 12, turn.

2nd row: P 4, turn.

3rd row: K 6, turn.

4th row: P 8, turn.

5th row: K 10, turn.

6th row: P 12, turn.

7th row: K 14, turn.

8th row: P 16, turn.

9th row: K to end.

St-st 7 more rows.

To shape the toe: *Next row:* (K 2 tog) to end – 10 sts.

Next row: (P 2 tog) to end – 5 sts. Break off yarn leaving a long end, thread it through remaining sts then pull up tightly and fasten off.

Join row ends then glue braid round the top of the stocking. Make a twisted cord as for the bauble and sew knot inside top edge of stocking.

To make Santa Claus

Body

Begin at lower edge and using red cast on 11 sts.

1st row: Inc K wise into every st – 22 sts. *

Beginning with a P row st-st 15 rows.

Break off red and join on pink for the head.

** St-st 11 rows.

Next row: (P 2 tog) to end – 11 sts. Break off yarn leaving a long end. Thread yarn loosely through remaining sts.

Gather round cast on edge and pull up tightly then fasten off. Join row ends then turn Santa right side out. Stuff firmly then pull up length of yarn tightly at top of head and fasten off. Tie a strand of yarn very tightly round the neck and sew the ends into body.

Glue a strip of braid round centre of body for a belt.

Arms [make two alike]

Using pink cast on 5 sts.

1st row: Inc K wise into every st – 10 sts.

P 1 row. Break off pink and join on red.

St-st 5 rows.

Next row: (P 2 tog) to end – 5 sts. Break off yarn leaving a long end. Thread yarn through remaining sts, pull up tightly and fasten off.

Now roll up the arm tightly across the width of the knitting and sew the edge in place. Sew arms to sides of body with gathered up sts at top near to neck and having the arms sloping slightly towards front of body.

Face

For each eye make a knot at the centre of a short length of black yarn. Use a darning needle to take the ends of the yarn through from the face to the back of the head keeping the knot vertical as shown in the diagram on page 42. Position the eyes half way down the face and leave two clear knitted sts between them. Knot ends of yarn securely at the back of head and sew ends into head. Make the nose in the same way from red yarn having the knot in horizontal position.

Hat

Using red cast on 28 sts. K 1 row. Now beginning with a K row st-st 4 rows.

Continue in st-st, dec 1 st at each end of every following row until 6 sts remain.

Next row: (P 2 tog) to end – 3 sts. Break off yarn leaving a long end and thread it through remaining sts then fasten off.

Join row ends. Make a twisted cord as for bauble, thread the ends of the cord through pointed top of hat and knot them on the inside. Sew the hat to Santa's head pushing a few loops of white yarn inside hat above the eyes for a fringe of hair.

Beard

Using white cast on 12 sts.

1st row: Inc K wise into every st – 24 sts.

Now work in g-st dec 1 st at each end of every row until 2 sts remain. K 2 tog then break off yarn and fasten off.

Sew cast on edge of beard to face as illustrated having sides meeting the hat. For the moustache make a couple of loops of white yarn around one finger and sew the centre of the loops below the nose. Sew the looped ends of moustache to the beard.

To make the snowman

Make the body and arms as for Santa using white yarn throughout.

Face

Make as for Santa using orange for the nose and working a small black stitch below nose for mouth.

Hat

Using blue cast on 28 sts. K 1 row.

Join on yellow and beginning with a K row st-st 10 rows, working in two row stripes of yellow and blue.

Next row: (K 2 tog) to end – 14 sts.

Next row: (P 2 tog) to end – 7 sts. Break off yarn and finish as for Santa's hat.

Make a twisted cord as for the bauble and sew the knot to top of snowman's head. Put hat on head and thread the cord up through the hat between the knitted sts. Sew hat to head.

Scarf

Using blue cast on 36 sts then cast off. Tie scarf round neck.

Broom

Make a tight twisted cord about 10 cm [4 in] in length using four strands of brown yarn. Knot the cord 3 cm [$1\frac{1}{4}$ in] away from folded end. Trim off yarn 2 cm [$\frac{3}{4}$ in] away from the knot and fray out ends for the bristles. Sew broom alongside one arm.

To make the angel

Make the body and arms as for Santa using pink for the head and hands and white for the body and arms. Sew arms in a praying position as illustrated.

Face

Work small V-shaped stitches for the eyes in black, splitting the yarn to give a finer strand. Work a small pink stitch for the mouth. Colour cheeks and position of nose with red pencil.

Hair

Using yellow yarn, make a hank measuring 16 cm [$6\frac{1}{4}$ in] across, winding yarn round 16 times. Open up the hank and sew the strands to position of centre parting above the eyes. Take strands to each side of head and sew there, then join them at centre back and sew there also. Now arrange remainder of hank to cover back of head, sewing the strands in place.

Make a small twist of yarn for the top of the head and also make a twisted cord as for the bauble. Sew twist of yarn in place tucking the knotted end of the cord underneath it at back of head.

Halo

Form a piece of gold braid into a 2.5 cm [1 in] diameter circle overlapping and gluing the ends. Catch a point on one edge of the halo to back of head.

Wings

Using white cast on 32 sts and work in g-st, dec 1 st at each end of every row until 4 sts remain. Cast off.

Gather up through the centre of the wings then sew to centre back of angel below neck. Catch wings to angel's back on either side of centre.

To make the choir boy

Body

Work as for Santa as far as *. Beginning with a P row st-st 6 rows. Break off red and join on white then st-st 9 rows. Break off white and join on pink for head. Continue working as for Santa from ** to the end. Make the arms as for Santa.

Hem of surplice

Using white cast on 26 sts. K 1 row then cast off. Sew the hem round the last row of the red portion at lower end of body.

Face

Work as for angel but with a vertical stitch for the mouth.

Hair

Using yellow cast on 24 sts. Beginning with a P row st-st 10 rows.

Next row: (P 2 tog) to end – 12 sts.

Break off yarn then finish off and make twisted cord etc. as for the snowman's hat on page 79, noting that P side of the work is the right side for the choir boy's hair.

Collar

Using white cast on 36 sts. K 1 row.

Next row: (K 2 tog) to end – 18 sts. Cast off. Place collar round neck oversewing row ends together at back of neck.

Song book

Using yellow cast on 8 sts, st-st 4 rows then cast off. Fold the book in half and press, then sew to the choir boy's hands as illustrated.

Santa and Mrs Claus

A pair of cheery Humpty Dumpty toys just right for the Christmas season! Knitted from two strands of double knitting yarn, they measure about 30 cm [12 in] from the tops of their hats to their toes.

You will need: Oddments of double knitting yarn in red, pink, white, green and black [note that it is advisable to have several balls of red yarn on hand when making these toys, but it does not matter if the shades vary]: a pair of $5\frac{1}{2}$mm [No 5] knitting needles and a pair of $3\frac{3}{4}$mm [No 9] knitting needles; small amount of stuffing for each toy; scraps of felt for facial features and the holly leaves.

Abbreviations: See page 17.

Important note: Please remember that the double knitting yarn is to be used *double* throughout and worked on $5\frac{1}{2}$mm [No 5] knitting needles. This is taken for granted in the instructions for each piece and so will not be mentioned again.

When single yarn and $3\frac{3}{4}$mm [No 9] needles are required [for the looped fringes] this will *always* be mentioned in the instructions.

Santa Claus

The body

Begin at lower edge and using red cast on 6 sts loosely then work as follows:

1st row: Inc K wise into every st – 12 sts.

2nd row: P.

3rd row: Inc K wise into every st – 24 sts.

Beginning with a P row st-st 3 rows.

Next row: Inc K wise into every st – 48 sts.

St-st 13 rows.

The head

Break off red and join on pink for head then continue in st-st and work 4 rows.

Next row: K 5, (K 2 tog, K 10) 3 times, K 2 tog, K 5 – 44 sts.

St-st 9 rows.

Next row: K 4, (K 2 tog, K 9) 3 times, K 2 tog, K 5 – 40 sts.

St-st 3 rows.

To shape top of head: *1st row:* (K 2, K 2 tog) to end – 30 sts.

2nd and every alternate row: P.

3rd row: (K 1, K 2 tog) to end – 20 sts.

5th row: (K 2 tog) to end – 10 sts.

7th row: (K 2 tog) to end – 5 sts.

Break off yarn leaving long ends, thread through remaining sts, then pull up tightly and fasten off.

The arms [make two alike]

Begin at top of arm and using red cast on 12 sts.

St-st 5 rows.

Break off red and join on white [read green here for Mrs Claus], then P 2 rows.

Next row: K.

Break off white [or green] and join on pink for hand.

Beginning with a K row, st-st 6 rows.

Next row: (K 2 tog) to end – 6 sts.

Break off yarn and finish off as for top of head.

The legs [make two alike]

Begin at top of leg and using red cast on 14 sts.

St-st 13 rows.

Break off red and join on white [read green here for Mrs Claus], then P 2 rows.

Next row: K.

Break off white [or green] and join on black for shoe.

Beginning with a K row, st-st 8 rows.

Next row: (K 2 tog) to end – 7 sts. Break off yarn and finish off as for top of head.

To make up Santa

Gather up the cast on sts of body tightly and fasten off, then join row ends of body leaving a small gap in head for turning. Turn right side out and stuff, then ladder stitch gap. Note that seam will be at centre back of toy.

Fold each arm and join the row ends leaving cast on edges open. Turn and stuff then oversew top edges together. Sew an arm to each side of body having top edge of arm level with last row of red on body and taking care that cast on edges of arms are in a vertical position as shown in the illustration.

Sew leg seams as for arms. Turn right side out and stuff lower portion of legs then stuff upper portions more lightly. Oversew top edges together having leg seams at centre back of legs. Sew legs to body at front having tops of legs two knitted rows up from last inc row at base of body, and in a horizontal position.

The face

Using a single strand of red yarn work a small V-shape for mouth about 2 cm [$\frac{3}{4}$ in] up from last row of red on body, securing end of yarn under position of one felt cheek [where it will be hidden] and fastening off yarn under position of other cheek. Using the pattern cut cheeks from pink felt and sew in place.

Cut nose from red felt and sew in place 1.5 cm [$\frac{5}{8}$ in] above mouth. Cut eyes from black felt and sew on either side of nose about 2 cm [$\frac{3}{4}$ in] apart.

The beard

Using $3\frac{3}{4}$ mm [No 9] needles and a single strand of white yarn, cast on 30 sts. Work looped pattern as follows.

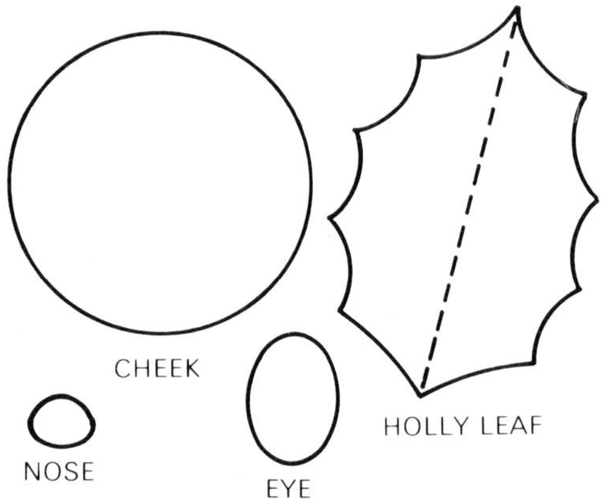

FULL SIZE PATTERNS

1st row: K 1; * insert right hand needle K wise into next st, place first two fingers of left hand at back of st, then wind yarn anticlockwise round needle and fingers 3 times, then round tip of right hand needle only, draw through the 4 loops; repeat from * until 1 st remains; K 1.

2nd row: K 1; * K 4 tog pulling loops down firmly as you go; repeat from * until 1 st remains; K 1 – 30 sts.

Cast off.

Pin, then sew beard to face as illustrated.

The hat

Note that the hat is worked in double yarn throughout, [including the looped lower edge], and on $5\frac{1}{2}$mm [No 5] needles.

Using white begin at lower edge and cast on 64 sts. Work the first row of the looped pattern as given for the beard, winding the yarn round needle and fingers twice instead of 3 times.

Break off white and join on red.

Work 2nd row of looped pattern: K 1; * K 3 tog pulling loops down firmly as you go, repeat from * until 1 st remains; K 1 – 64 sts.

Now beginning with a P row, st-st 9 rows.

** **Shape the top:** *Next row:* (K 2, K 2 tog) to end – 48 sts.

St-st 3 rows.

Next row: (K 1, K 2 tog) to end – 32 sts.

St-st 3 rows.

Next row: (K 2 tog) to end – 16 sts. ***

St-st 3 rows.

Next row: (K 2 tog) to end – 8 sts.

Break off yarn leaving long ends, thread through remaining sts, pull up tightly and fasten off. Join row ends of hat.

Make a pom-pon in white yarn and sew to top of hat. Place hat on head as illustrated and sew to head through first row of red sts. Cut two holly leaves from green felt using the pattern. Work stitches up the centre of each one, then sew them to hat as shown in illustration.

Mrs Claus

Work body and head in exactly the same way as given for Santa.

Make arms and legs as for Santa noting variations in colour.

Make up all pieces and cut out and sew on facial features as for Santa.

The skirt

Using $3\frac{3}{4}$ mm [No 9] needles and a single strand of red yarn cast on 70 sts.

Work the two rows of the looped pattern as given for Santa's beard, winding the yarn round three fingers instead of two, to make longer loops. Join row ends of skirt and sew it round body just below the arms.

The hair

Use white yarn and wind it 30 times around a 40 cm [16 in] length of card. Take this hank of yarn off card and sew across strands at centre of hank. Sew centre, to centre parting position on head, starting 2 cm [$\frac{3}{4}$ in] above the eyes.

Gather strands to each side of head just above the arms and sew there. Take ends of loops up towards centre back of head and sew in place.

The hat

Begin at lower edge and using green cast on 128 sts.

G-st 4 rows.

Next row: (K 2 tog) to end – 64 sts.

Beginning with a P row, st-st 13 rows.

Now work as for Santa's hat from ** to ***.

Next row: (P 2 tog) to end – 8 sts.

Break off yarn leaving long ends and finish and sew seam as for Santa, omitting pom-pon.

Put a little stuffing in top of hat, then put hat on head as shown in the illustration. Sew hat to head through the dec row after the first 4 rows of g-st.

The super seven

All these toys are very quick and easy to make. The animals are knitted with two strands of double knitting yarn and you can make the baby dolls from the same pattern using one strand of yarn.

Lion, tiger, panda, teddy and piglet are all roughly 25 cm [10 in] tall, while the dolls measure just 18 cm [7 in].

For the animals you will need: Oddments of double knitting yarn in assorted colours as shown in the illustration [note that because lion is worked all in one colour, you will need a 50 g ball of yarn to complete it]; a pair of 5 mm [No 6] knitting needles; small amount of stuffing for each animal; scraps of felt for facial features; dark brown permanent marker pen; a red pencil; adhesive.
For the baby dolls you will need: Oddments of double knitting yarn in assorted colours as shown in the illustration; a pair of $3\frac{1}{4}$ mm [No 10] knitting needles; small amount of stuffing; scraps of black felt; tiny guipure flower trimming; a red pencil; adhesive.

Abbreviations: See page 17.

Note: The animals' legs, bodies, heads and arms are all worked in the same basic way except for changing colours to give the effect of trousers, etc.

Important note: Please remember that the double knitting yarn is to be used double throughout for *all* the animal pieces, except for the lion's mane where yarn is used single. This is taken for granted in the instructions for each piece and so will not be mentioned again.

Work any facial embroidered stitches with single yarn.

The lion

Legs

Using yellow begin at lower edge of one leg and cast on 8 sts.

1st row: Inc K wise into every st – 16 sts **.

Now beginning with a P row st-st 17 rows.

Break off yarn and leave sts on a spare needle then work another leg in same way.

Body

Having right side of work facing, K across both sets of leg sts – 32 sts.

Now beginning with a P row, st-st 13 rows.
*** **To shape the shoulders:** *Next row:* K 6, (K 2 tog) twice, K 12, (K 2 tog) twice, K 6 – 28 sts.

St-st 3 rows ****.
Dec for neck: *Next row:* K 5, (K 2 tog) twice, K 10, (K 2 tog) twice, K 5 – 24 sts.

P 1 row.
Inc for head: *Next row:* (K 1, inc in next st) to end – 36 sts.

Continue in st-st and work 19 rows.
Shape top of head: *Next row:* K 7, (K 2 tog) twice, K 14, (K 2 tog) twice, K 7 – 32 sts.

P 1 row.

Next row: K 6, (K 2 tog) twice, K 12, (K 2 tog) twice, K 6 – 28 sts.

Next row: (P 2 tog) to end – 14 sts.

Next row: (K 2 tog) to end – 7 sts.

Break off yarn leaving long ends and thread through remaining sts, then pull up tightly and fasten off.

Arms [make two alike]

Using yellow begin at lower end of arm and cast on 7 sts.

1st row: Inc K wise into every st – 14 sts **.

Now beginning with a P row, st-st 11 rows.

*** Shape top of arm by dec 1 st at each end of next and every following alternate row until 6 sts remain

Cast off.

Ears [make two alike]

Using yellow cast on 5 sts.

1st row: Inc K wise into every st – 10 sts.

Beginning with a P row st-st 3 rows.
Next row: (K 2 tog) to end – 5 sts.
P 1 row.
Next row: Inc K wise into every st – 10 sts.
St-st 3 rows.
Next row: (K 2 tog) to end – 5 sts.
Cast off.

The mane

Using 1 strand of pale yellow cast on 50 sts.

Next row: K 1; * insert right hand needle K wise into next st, place first two fingers of left hand at back of st, then wind yarn anti-clockwise round needle and fingers 3 times, then round tip of right hand needle once, draw through the 4 loops; repeat from * until 1 st remains, K 1.

Next row: K 1, * K 4 tog, pulling loops down firmly as you go; repeat from * until 1 st remains, K 1 – 50 sts.

Cast off.

To make up lion

Join row ends of body and head from tops of legs leaving a gap in body seam. Join row ends of each leg then oversew across cast on edges at lower edges of legs.

Turn lion right side out and stuff, then ladder stitch gap in seam. Tie a length of matching yarn very tightly round body at position of neck decrease row.

Join row ends of arms leaving top shaped edges open then oversew across cast on edges at lower edges of arms. Turn right side out and stuff, then sew open edges of arms to sides of body having cast off edges of arms level with neck.

Join row ends of mane strip and pin around face as shown in the illustration. Sew cast off edge in place then sew mane to face again through the knitted row at top of loops.

For the mouth work a 2.5 cm [1 in] vertical stitch in black yarn from centre of face downwards, then work a V-shape at base of this stitch. Cut nose from dark brown felt, and eyes from black felt using the patterns. Stick them in place as illustrated.

Fold each ear bringing cast on and cast off edges together then join row ends at each side. Turn right side out and oversew cast on and cast off edges together. Sew ears to mane as illustrated, placing them about 4.5 cm [$1\frac{3}{4}$ in] apart.

The panda

Legs, body, head and arms

Work as given for the lion using black for the legs then changing to white for working the body and head.

Work the arms in black.

Ears [make two alike]

Using black cast on 6 sts.
1st row: Inc K wise into every st – 12 sts.
Beginning with a P row st-st 3 rows.
Next row: (K 2 tog) to end – 6 sts.
P 1 row.
Next row: Inc K wise into every st – 12 sts.
St-st 3 rows.
Next row: (K 2 tog) to end – 6 sts.
Cast off.

The skirt

Using red begin at hem edge and cast on 48 sts.

G-st 2 rows.

Now beginning with a K row, st-st 8 rows.

Dec for waist: *Next row:* (K 1, K 2 tog) to end – 32 sts.

Cast off loosely.

The straps [make two alike]

Using red cast on 24 sts then cast off.

To make up panda

Make up body, arms and ears as for lion. Sew ears to top of head at front placing them about 6 cm [$2\frac{1}{2}$ in] apart.

Make a short pink stitch for mouth about 2 cm [$\frac{3}{4}$ in] up from neck. Cut nose from red felt using the pattern and stick it to centre of face. Cut eye pieces from black and white felt as indicated on pattern on page 86. Glue them together as shown then stick to face.

Oversew row ends of skirt together then put skirt on panda with seam at centre back. Place straps over shoulders crossing them over at back. Tuck and pin ends of straps inside waist edge of skirt. Sew waist edge of skirt to panda, catching in straps when sewing.

The tiger

Legs, body, head and arms

Work as for lion's legs and body in two row stripes of brown and orange as far as ****. After this continue in orange only.

Work arms as for lion in two row stripes to match tiger's body.

Ears [make two alike]

Using orange cast on 10 sts.

Beginning with a K row, st-st 2 rows.

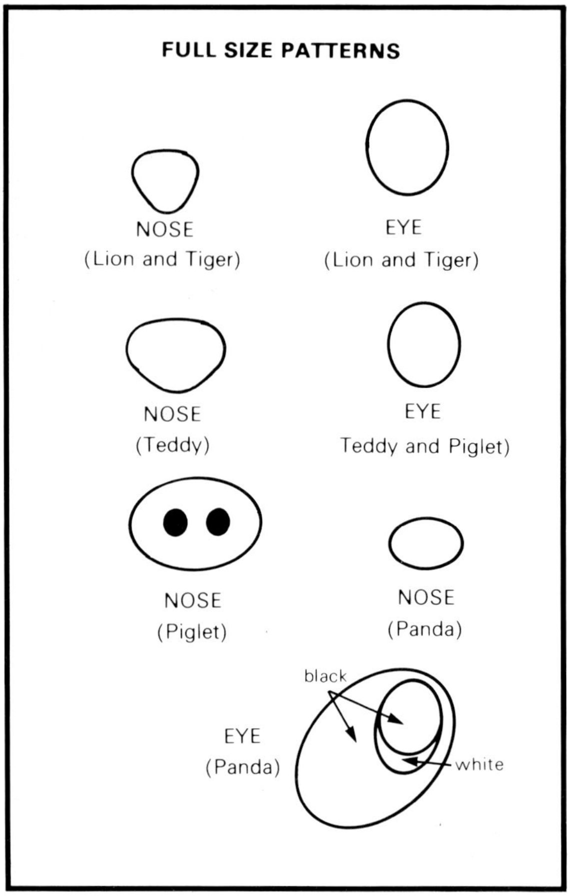

Continue in st-st dec 1 st at each end of next and every following alternate row until 4 sts remain.

P 1 row then inc 1 st at each end of next and every following alternate row until there are 10 sts.

P 1 row then cast off.

To make up tiger

Make up body, arms and ears as for lion. Sew ears to head about 4 cm [$1\frac{1}{2}$ in] apart. Add mouth, nose and eyes as for lion.

Now using brown marker pen, mark face with stripes as shown in the illustration, blotting the markings with paper tissue as they are made. Mark back of head with irregular stripes also.

The teddy

Legs

Using tan work as for lion as far as **.

Now beginning with a P row, st-st 5 rows.

Break off tan and join on black and white [one strand of black and one of white for the tweedy effect].

St-st 12 rows.

Break off yarn and leave sts on a spare needle then work another leg in same way.

Body

Having right side of work facing, continue in leg colours and K across both sets of legs sts – 32 sts.

St-st 7 rows.

Break off yarn and join on orange then st-st 2 rows.

Break off orange and join on blue then st-st 4 rows.

Continue in blue working as for lion from *** to ****.

Break off blue and join on tan then continue in tan as for lion from **** to end.

Arms [make two alike]

Using tan work as for lion as far as **.

Now beginning with a P row, st-st 5 rows.

Break off tan and join on blue then st-st 6 rows.

Now work as for lion's arm from *** to end.

Ears [make two alike]

Using tan work as given for panda's ears.

To make up teddy

Make up body, arms and ears as for lion. Sew ears to head as for panda.

For mouth work a 1 cm [$\frac{3}{8}$ in] black stitch from centre of face downwards then work a shallow W at base of this stitch.

Cut eyes and nose from black felt using the patterns then stick them in place.

The piglet

Legs, body and head

Work as for the lion as far as ****, using pink for the legs and changing to blue for the body.
Break off blue and join on pink then work as for lion from **** to end.

Arms [make two alike]

Work as for teddy beginning with pink then changing to blue for sleeve colour.

Ears [make two alike]

Using pink work as for tiger's ears.

Skirt and straps

Make as for panda's skirt using deep pink.

To make up piglet

Make up body, arms and ears as for lion. Sew ears to head pointing them forward slightly onto face and spacing them 4 cm [$1\frac{1}{2}$ in] apart. Make up and sew on skirt as for panda.
Work a V-shape in red for mouth 2.5 cm [1 in] up from neck. Cut nose from deep pink felt using the pattern on page 86 and mark nostrils in red pencil. Cut eyes from black felt using the pattern then glue eyes and nose in place. Colour cheeks with red pencil.

The baby dolls

Important note: The dolls are worked in one strand of double knitting yarn only, using the same basic pattern as the animals.

To make legs, body and head

Using pink or blue yarn, work legs and body as for lion as far as ****.
Break off yarn; join on pale pink for head.
Work as for lion from **** to end.

Arms [make two alike]

Using pale pink begin at lower end of arm and cast on 7 sts.
1st row: Inc K wise into every st – 14 sts.
Now beginning with a P row, st-st 5 rows.
Break off pale pink and join on pink or blue.
St-st 6 rows.
Shape top of arm by dec 1 st at each end of next and every following alternate row until 6 sts remain.
Cast off.

Hat

Using pink or blue cast on 40 sts and work in single rib for 4 rows.
Beginning with a K row st-st 16 rows.
Shape top of hat: *Next row:* (K 2 tog) to end – 20 sts.
P 1 row.
Next row: (K 2 tog) to end.
Break off yarn leaving a long end then thread it through remaining sts, pull up tightly and fasten off.

To make up doll

Make up body, arms etc. in same way as for the animals.
For the mouth work a short stitch in deep pink 1.5 cm [$\frac{1}{2}$ in] above neck. For eyes cut tiny circles of black felt (use a leather punch, if available, to cut these). Stick eyes to face 3 cm [$1\frac{1}{8}$ in] above neck and 2 cm [$\frac{3}{4}$ in] apart. Colour cheeks with red pencil.
Join row ends of hat and turn right side out. Make a small pom-pon and sew to top. Pull hat onto doll's head as illustrated with seam at back. Cut a few short lengths of yellow yarn and tie them together at centre. Tease out strands with a comb or brush. Push tied centre of strands under hat at front. Trim ends of strands as necessary. Now sew hat to head all round cast on edge.
Sew three guipure flowers to front of body as shown in the illustration.

The scarecrow

Children and adults alike will love this friendly character. Measuring about 34 cm [13½ in] in height, he is knitted in a mixture of stocking stitch and garter stitch and comes complete with companions – mouse, robin and ladybird. The scarecrow is also featured on the front and back covers of this book.

You will need: For the jacket, two 20 g balls of blue double knitting yarn or colour of your choice; for the rest of the toy, oddments of double knitting yarn in assorted colours as shown in the illustration; a pair of 3 mm [No 11] knitting needles; stuffing; scraps of blue and black felt for the eyes; a red pencil; adhesive.

Abbreviations: See page 17.

Pants, body and head

Pants pieces [make two alike]
These are knitted sideways so that the stripes are vertical on the finished toy. Note that P side of knitting is the right side, when making up the pants.

Using black cast on 26 sts and st-st 2 rows. Join on grey and st-st 2 rows using grey.

Repeat the last 4 rows 9 more times, carrying strands of yarn loosely up the side of the work. Cast off loosely.

Join the pants pieces to each other at one cast on and cast off edge for 12 sts only, to form the centre front seam of the pants as shown in diagram 1 on page 92. Mark the other cast on and cast off edges with coloured threads 12 sts down from the waist edge, also as shown in diagram 1. At this stage the pants pieces will appear to be rather short, but they will stretch to the correct length when made up and stuffed.

Body and head
Begin at waist edge of body and using red cast on 50 sts.

St-st 16 rows.

Dec to shape shoulders: *Next row:* K 7, (K 2 tog) 6 times, K 12, (K 2 tog) 6 times, K 7 – 38 sts.

P 1 row then break off red and join on cream for head.

St-st 2 rows.

Inc to shape the head: *Next row:* K 10, inc into each of next 18 sts, K 10 – 56 sts.

St-st 35 rows.

Dec to shape top of head: *Next row:* (K 2 tog) to end – 28 sts.

P 1 row.

Next row: (K 2 tog) to end – 14 sts. Break off yarn leaving a long end then thread it loosely through remaining sts and leave.

To make up pants body and head pieces
Mark centre of cast on edge of body with a coloured thread. Now oversew this edge to waist edge of pants pieces, matching coloured thread on body to centre front seam on pants. Join row ends of head and body, leaving a gap in body seam for turning and stuffing, then join pants pieces from waist edge as far as coloured threads. Now bring cast on and cast off edges of each pants piece together and join these to form pants legs.

Turn scarecrow right side out and stuff body and lower portion of head through gap in body seam. Ladder stitch the gap. To shape the neck, use a double strand of cream yarn and gather round first knitted row of cream on the head. Pull up the gathers very tightly and knot ends of yarn then sew ends into neck.

Now continue stuffing head through opening at top. Pull up length of yarn tightly then fasten off. Stuff legs through lower edges of pants allowing them to stretch to length as you stuff.

Boots [make two alike]

Begin at lower edge of sole and using black cast on 26 sts.

1st row: Inc K wise into every st – 52 sts.

Beginning with a P row, st-st 5 rows. Break off black and join on tan then st-st 8 rows.

Dec to shape top of boot: *Next row:* K 10, (K 2 tog) 16 times, K 10 – 36 sts.

P 1 row.

Next row: K 8, (K 2 tog) 10 times, K 8 – 26 sts.
St-st 2 rows then cast off.

Join row ends of boot then oversew across cast on edge. Turn right side out and stuff. Lap and pin lower edges of pants legs just over cast off edges of boots having toes of boots pointing away from each other as shown in the illustration. Slip stitch pants to boots as pinned pushing in more stuffing as necessary to make ankles firm.

Face

Use a strand of red yarn for mouth. Work an uneven V-shape with a small gap at centre, having lower point of the V six knitted sts up from the head inc row. Work a small stitch at each corner of the mouth.

Cut two pupils from black felt and two eyes from blue felt using the patterns on page 92. Stick the pieces together in pairs then glue eyes to face 2 cm [$\frac{3}{4}$ in] up from corners of the mouth placing them 2.5 cm [1 in] apart.

Carrot nose

Using orange cast on 8 sts. St-st 2 rows.

Continuing in st-st, dec 1 st at each end of next row then on the following alternate row – 4 sts.

P 1 row.

Next row: (K 2 tog) twice – 2 sts.

Break off yarn leaving a long end and thread it through remaining sts, pull up tightly and fasten off. Oversew row ends together having P side of knitting on the inside. Turn nose right side out and stuff, then sew to face as illustrated. Colour cheeks with red pencil.

Hat and hair

Hat crown

Using light green cast on 72 sts. G-st 30 rows.
Dec to shape top: *Next row:* (K 2, K 2 tog) to end – 54 sts.

G-st 3 rows.

Next row: (K 1, K 2 tog) to end – 36 sts.

K 1 row.

Next row: (K 2 tog) to end – 18 sts.

Break off yarn leaving a long end then thread it through remaining sts, pull up tightly and fasten off.

Hat brim

Using light green cast on 126 sts. G-st 14 rows.

Next row: (K 5, K 2 tog) to end – 108 sts.

Next row: (K 1, K 2 tog) to end – 72 sts. Cast off.

Hat band

Using red cast on 74 sts. K 1 row then cast off.

Hair

Using yellow cast on 72 sts.

1st row: K 1; * insert right hand needle K wise into next st, place first 2 fingers of left hand at back of st, wind yarn anti-clockwise round needle and fingers twice, then round tip of right hand needle only, draw through the 3 loops; repeat from * until 1 st remains, K 1.

Next [dec and cast off] row: K 1; * K 3 tog pulling loops down firmly as you go, pass first st on right hand needle over second st thus casting it off; repeat from * to last st, K 1 then cast off last st.

To make up hat and hair

Join row ends of hat crown piece for 1 cm [$\frac{3}{8}$ in] in from each end. Join row ends of hat brim. Now oversew cast off edge of brim to cast on edge of crown noting that seam of hat crown will be at front of scarecrow providing gap for inserting mouse later on.

Join row ends of hair and clip through all the loops to form single strands. Now using matching sewing thread, machine stitch through the knitted loops at the cast off edge to ensure that individual strands of yarn can not be pulled out. If you do not have a sewing machine then make sure that all the loops are caught and sewn in place when attaching the hair to the hat brim.

Oversew cast off edge of hair to cast off edge of brim. Place completed hat on head as shown in the illustration and catch it to head through lower edge of crown. Now join row ends of hat band and sew it round lower edge of crown.

Belt

Using dark green cast on 50 sts and st-st 5 rows then cast off.

Oversew row ends together then put belt on scarecrow placing seam at back and having upper edge of belt lapping over first row of red on body. Sew in place.

Buckle

Using yellow cast on 26 sts then cast off.

Oversew row ends together then sew buckle to front of belt as shown in illustration.

Bow tie

Using pale blue cast on 36 sts then cast off.

Form into a bow shape and sew to front of chest under chin.

Sleeves and mittens

Sleeves [make two alike]
Begin at wrist edge and using blue cast on 22 sts.

G-st 26 rows

To shape top: Dec 1 st at each end of next and every following alternate row until 6 sts remain. Cast off.

Mittens [make two alike]
Begin at wrist edge and using grey cast on 20 sts.

St-st 4 rows.

To shape thumb: Inc 1 st at each end of next 3 rows – 26 sts.

St-st 3 rows then dec 1 st at each end of next row – 24 sts.

Next row: P 3 tog, P 18, P 3 tog – 20 sts.

St-st 7 rows.

Next row: (P 2 tog) to end – 10 sts.

Cast off P wise.

To make up
Oversew row ends of each sleeve together except for shaped portion at top. Turn right side out. Join row ends of each mitten and oversew across cast off sts. Turn right side out and stuff.

Oversew cast on edges of sleeves to cast on edges of mittens, making sure that thumbs will be pointing upwards when sleeves are sewn in place. Stuff sleeves then sew the open edges to sides of scarecrow placing cast off edges of sleeves 1 cm [$\frac{3}{8}$ in] down from neck.

Coat

Fronts [make two pieces alike]
Begin at shoulder edge and using blue cast on 16 sts.

G-st 30 rows.

Mark each end of last row with coloured thread.

G-st a further 24 rows **.

Cast off.

Back [make two pieces alike]
Work as for fronts as far as **.

To shape coat tail: *Next row:* K to last 3 sts, K 2 tog, K 1.

Next row: K.

Repeat these 2 rows 12 more times – 3 sts.

Next row: K 3 tog, then fasten off.

Buttons [make four alike]
Using pale blue cast on 12 sts.

Next row: (K 2 tog) to end – 6 sts.

Break off yarn leaving a long end, thread it through remaining sts, then pull up tightly and fasten off.

To make up the coat
Oversew the long straight row ends of coat back pieces together from the cast on edges for 10 cm [4 in] as shown in diagram 2 on page 92.

Now oversew the coat front pieces to back pieces at sides below the coloured threads

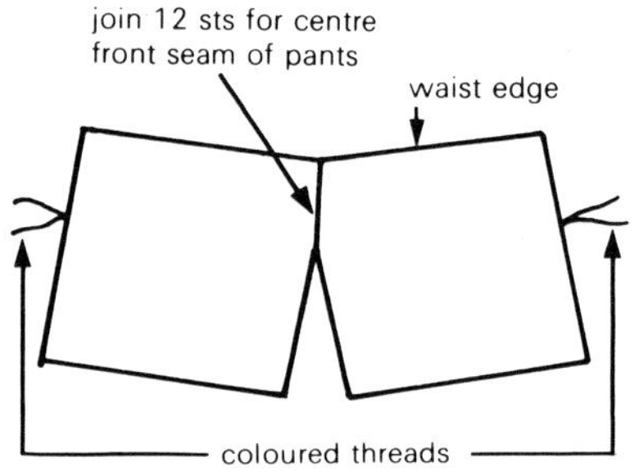

DIAGRAM 1
Joining front seam on pants piece

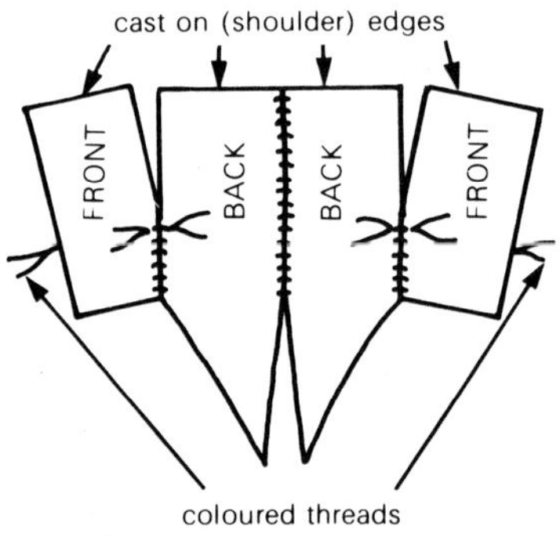

DIAGRAM 2
Joining back and side seams on coat

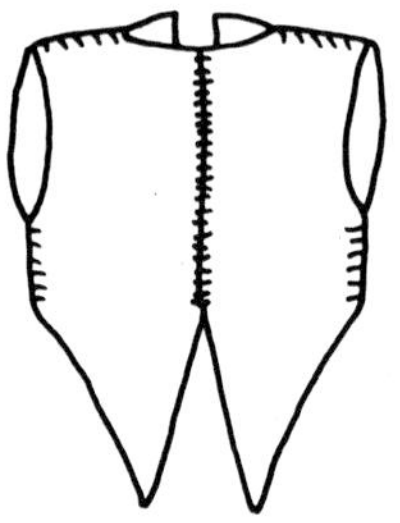

DIAGRAM 3
Joining shoulder edges of coat pieces

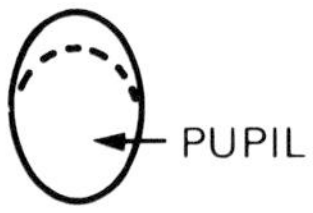

FULL-SIZE PATTERN
For eye and pupil

only, leaving the rows above coloured threads open for the armholes as shown in diagram 2.

Oversew the shoulder edges of front and back pieces together for 2.5 cm [1 in] as shown in diagram 3. Turn coat right side out.

Put coat on scarecrow and slip stitch the armhole edges to the sleeves. Fold back the upper corners of fronts to form lapels then catch them in place. Oversew row ends of each button then sew two buttons to right front of coat and one on each side of centre back seam at waist level. Work a cross stitch in black at centre of each button and two straight black stitches on left front of coat for buttonholes.

Ankle fringes [make two alike]

Using yellow cast on 34 sts. Work in same way as given for hair, but wind yarn round one finger instead of two. Join row ends of fringe and clip through all loops. Machine stitch etc. as for hair. Slip stitch fringes in place round ankles.

Wrist fringes [make two alike]

Using yellow cast on 26 sts. Work and sew in place etc. as for ankle fringes.

Flower in lapel

Stalk and leaves: Using light green cast on 28 sts then cast off.
Flower: Using yellow cast on 20 sts.
1st row: (K 2 tog) to end – 10 sts.
2nd row: (K 2 tog) to end – 5 sts.

Break off yarn leaving a long end then thread it through remaining sts, pull up tightly and fasten off. Oversew row ends of flower together and work a few stitches in green at centre of flower.

Form one end of the green strip into two loops for the leaf shapes leaving the other end for the stalk. Sew this piece to back of flower then sew flower to left lapel.

Robin

Using brown and beginning at lower edge cast on 8 sts.

1st row: Inc K wise into every st – 16 sts.
Beginning with a K row work in st-st shaping tail end of body by inc 1 st at each end of next 3 rows – 22 sts.
St-st 3 rows.
Next row: K 3 tog, K 16, K 3 tog – 18 sts.
Next row: P 3 tog, P 12, P 3 tog – 14 sts.
To shape neck: *Next row:* K 5, (K 2 tog) twice, K 5 – 12 sts.
St-st 4 rows for head.
Next row: (P 2 tog) to end – 6 sts.
Break off yarn leaving a long end then thread it through remaining sts, pull up tightly and fasten off. Oversew row ends together leaving cast on edges open. Turn right side out and stuff.
Using a strand of black yarn, work dots for eyes and a double loop of yarn for beak, securing ends of yarn in stuffing at lower edge. Put a dab of adhesive on the beak loops and pinch into a pointed shape. Gather round the cast on sts, pull up tightly and fasten off.

Breast

Using red cast on 3 sts.
1st row: Inc K wise into every st – 6 sts.
Beginning with a P row, st-st 5 rows ***.
Next row: (K 2 tog) to end – 3 sts. Cast off.
Sew breast to front of robin's chest.

Wings [make two alike]

Using brown work as for breast as far as ***.
St-st 5 more rows.
Next row: (P 2 tog) to end – 3 sts.
Break off yarn leaving a long end then thread through remaining sts, pull up tightly and fasten off. Sew wings to sides of robin having cast on edges level with sides of breast.

Tail

Using brown cast on 6 sts and st-st 5 rows.
Next row: (P 2 tog) to end – 3 sts. Cast off.
Sew cast off edge to tail end of body.

Feet

The foot stitches are worked on the scarecrow's sleeve using fawn yarn. Work three stitches for each foot, fanning out from a centre point, and having feet side by side. Sew robin in place on the scarecrow's sleeve so that feet are visible in front of the robin's breast.

Mouse

Begin at tail end and using fawn cast on 12 sts, leaving a long end of yarn for making the tail later on.
St-st 12 rows.
To shape head: Dec 1 st at each end of next 4 rows – 4 sts.
Break off yarn leaving a long end and thread it through remaining sts, pull up tightly and fasten off. Oversew row ends together leaving cast on edge open. Turn right side out and stuff. Work eyes as for robin and a couple of stitches for nose.
For the ears double fawn yarn and work two small loops behind the eyes. To hold these loops in place sew them to head at lower edge with sewing thread.
Gather round the cast on sts, pull up tightly and fasten off. Twist yarn for tail and allow it to curl up tightly, making the tail 7 cm [3 in] in length. Sew in the end of yarn.
Put the mouse inside the gap at front of scarecrow's hat and sew it to the head.

Ladybird

Using red cast on 3 sts.
1st row: Inc K wise into every st – 6 sts.
St-st 4 rows.
Break off red and join on black then st-st 2 rows.
Next row: (K 2 tog) to end – 3 sts.
Break off yarn leaving a long end. Thread it through remaining sts then gather all round edges of knitted piece. Pull up gathers tightly stuffing the centre, then fasten off.
Work a line in black yarn down the centre of body then work a black spot on either side of this line. For the eyes work small white stitches using sewing thread. Sew the ladybird to the toe of the scarecrow's boot.

The witty knits

A dozen irresistable little toys, cheerful enough to brighten anyone's day and all based on one easy pattern. Suitable as soft toys for children or mascots for the young at heart; they stand just 9 cm [$3\frac{1}{2}$ in] high, excluding the hats.

For Hallowe'en there is a ghost, a witch and a scarecrow complete with pumpkin. Instructions are given for including a rattle in the toys if you wish and children will particularly enjoy the ghost, rattling his chains!

You will need: Oddments of double knitting yarn in assorted colours as shown in the illustrations; a pair of 3 mm [No 11] knitting needles; oddment of Twilley's silver Goldfingering yarn [or you can use silver gift wrapping cord as an alternative]; small amount of stuffing; a crochet hook [any size will do]; scraps of felt to match the yarn used for the bodies; for the rattles, empty [normal size] matchboxes and sticky tape plus small bells, dried peas or lentils etc.; a red pencil.

Abbreviations: See page 17.

Note: Instructions for including the rattle and for making up the basic toy are given for the ghost only. Refer to these instructions if you wish to include a rattle in any of the other toys.

The ghost

The body

Begin at lower edge and using white cast on 60 sts, marking the exact centre of the cast on row with a coloured thread.

1st row: (K 2 tog) to end – 30 sts.

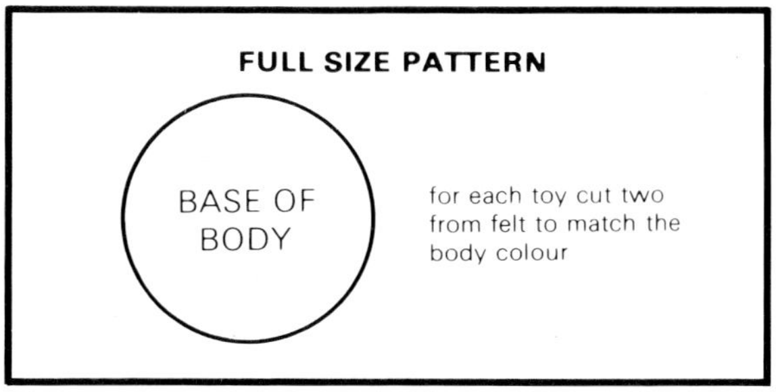

Beginning with a K row, st-st 20 rows.

To shape the neck: *Next row:* K 6, (K 2 tog) 3 times, K 6, (K 2 tog) 3 times, K 6 – 24 sts.

St-st 10 rows.

Next row: (P 2 tog) to end – 12 sts. Break off yarn leaving a long end.

Thread it through remaining sts, pull up tightly and fasten off.

The arms [make two alike]

Begin at top of arm and using white cast on 18 sts.

1st row: (P 2 tog) to end – 9 sts.

Beginning with a K row, st-st 8 rows. Break off yarn and finish off as for the body.

The ball and chain

For the ball, wind a 2 cm [$\frac{3}{4}$ in] diameter ball of black yarn. Thread a darning needle with the end of yarn and take it back and forth through the ball to secure the wound strands. Lightly press the ball by rolling it about under a warm iron.

Crochet a 50 cm [20 in] long loose chain using silver yarn. Attach one end of the chain to the ball.

The rattle

Only the tray portion of the matchbox is required to make the rattle. Cut the tray in half along the length then cut these pieces in half across the width. Use two of these four pieces to form a box, enclosing materials for the rattle as suggested.

Note that for the ghost, a couple of small bells make a sound nearest to that of rattling chains. Secure and seal the edges of the box with sticky tape.

To make up the ghost

Join the row ends of the body then turn right side out. Stuff the head, then the body. If you wish to include a rattle, place it at the centre of the body and pack the stuffing around it.

Now sew the point marked with coloured thread on the cast on row, to the centre back at the seam. To contain the stuffing at the open lower edges, cut two base pieces from felt to match the body colour, using the pattern. Slip these circles inside the lower edges and slip stitch them in place at the first [decrease] row on the body.

Join the row ends of each arm, turn right side out and stuff. Sew the arms to sides of body having seams underneath the arms and top edges level with the neck shaping sts.

For the mouth use black yarn and work two stitches to form a V-shape, having centre of the V two knitted sts up from the neck and upper points of the V two knitted sts apart (see illustration on page 99).

For each eye use black yarn and work a small chain stitch, then work another chain stitch on top of, and covering the first one. Position the eyes 1 cm [$\frac{3}{8}$ in] apart and 1 cm [$\frac{3}{8}$ in] above the mouth.

When making up the other toys, mark a small dot for the nose between the eyes and colour the cheeks also, with red pencil.

Loop the chain and sew to the ghost's hands as shown in the illustration.

The witch

The body

Begin at lower edge and using green cast on 60 sts, marking the exact centre of the cast on row with a coloured thread.

1st row: (K 2 tog) to end – 30 sts.

Beginning with a K row, st-st 20 rows. Break off green and join on pink.

To shape the neck: *Next row:* K 6, (K 2 tog) 3 times, K 6, (K 2 tog) 3 times, K 6 – 24 sts.

St-st 10 rows.

Next row: (P 2 tog) to end – 12 sts. Break off yarn leaving a long end. Thread it through remaining sts, pull up tightly and fasten off.

The arms [make two alike]

Begin at top of arm and using green cast on 18 sts.

1st row: (P 2 tog) to end – 9 sts. Beginning with a K row, st-st 5 rows. Break off green and join on pink then st-st 3 rows. Break off yarn and finish off as for the body.

The hat brim

Using black cast on 48 sts and g-st 4 rows.

Next row: (K 2 tog) to end – 24 sts.

Cast off loosely.

The hat top

Using black cast on 24 sts loosely and st-st 4 rows.

Shape top: *Next row:* (K 1, K 2 tog) to end – 16 sts.

St-st 5 rows.

Next row: (K 2 tog) to end – 8 sts.

St-st 3 rows.

Next row: (K 2 tog) to end – 4 sts.

Break off yarn leaving a long end. Thread this through remaining sts, pull up tightly and fasten off.

The broomstick

For the handle make a tightly twisted cord from four strands of brown yarn, making the handle 7 cm [$2\frac{3}{4}$ in] in length. To stiffen the handle, wind a strand of brown yarn very tightly round it, working from one end to the other, then back again. Sew ends of yarn into the handle.

For the bristles, tie a bunch of brown yarn strands round one end of the handle with sewing thread, then fray out ends of yarn.

To make up the witch

Make up the body and arms and add facial features as for the ghost [see above].

Oversew the row ends of the hat brim together then press it flat with a warm iron. For the hair cut a few 12 cm [$4\frac{3}{4}$ in] lengths of black yarn. Fray them out and then sew the centres to top of witch's head. Space out the strands to hang down sides of face and back of head. Place the hat brim on the head and sew inner edge in place. Join the row ends of the hat top, turn right side out and stuff, then sew the cast on edge to inner edge of the hat brim.

Make a bow from a strand of red yarn and sew to front of witch. Sew broomstick to one hand.

The scarecrow

The body

Begin at lower edge and using blue tweedy yarn cast on 60 sts, marking the exact centre of the cast on row with a coloured thread.

1st row: (K 2 tog) to end – 30 sts.

Beginning with a K row, st-st 12 rows. Break off blue and join on red then st-st 8 rows. Break off red and join on pink.

To shape the neck: *Next row:* K 6, (K 2 tog) 3 times, K 6, (K 2 tog) 3 times, K 6 – 24 sts.

St-st 10 rows.

Next row: (P 2 tog) to end – 12 sts.

Break off yarn leaving a long end. Thread it through remaining sts, pull up tightly and fasten off.

The arms [make two alike]

Begin at top of arm and using red cast on 18 sts.

1st row: (P 2 tog) to end – 9 sts. Beginning with a K row, st-st 5 rows. Break off red and join on black then st-st 3 rows. Break off yarn and finish off as for the body.

The hat brim

Using brown cast on 48 sts and g-st 4 rows.

Next row: (K 2 tog) to end – 24 sts.

Cast off loosely.

The hat top

Using brown cast on 24 sts and g-st 6 rows.

Shape top: *Next row:* (K 2 tog) to end – 12 sts.

Next row: (K 2 tog) to end – 6 sts. Break off yarn leaving a long end. Thread this through remaining sts, pull up tightly and fasten off.

The scarf

Using green cast on 60 sts then cast off.

The pumpkin

Using orange cast on 15 sts.

1st row: Inc K wise into every st – 30 sts.

Beginning with a K row, st-st 18 rows.

Next row: (K 2 tog) to end – 15 sts. Break off yarn leaving a 1 m [1 yd] length. Thread end of yarn loosely through remaining sts.

For the stalk use green and cast on 6 sts.

St-st 4 rows then cast off.

To make up the scarecrow

Make up the body and arms and add facial features as for the ghost [see opposite].

Oversew the row ends of the hat brim together. For the hair cut a few 9 cm [$3\frac{1}{2}$ in] lengths of yellow yarn then sew them together at centres then sew centres to top of head. Fray out the ends of yarn and space them out evenly all round the head. Place the hat brim on head and sew inner edge in place. Trim the ends of the hair. Oversew row ends of hat top together, turn right side out, then sew cast on edge to inner edge of hat brim.

Tie a strand of blue yarn round the hat for a hat band. Tie scarf round neck and sew in place. Work darns with yarn on the body as shown in the illustration.

Roll up the pumpkin stalk across the width and sew row ends in place. Gather up the cast on edge of the pumpkin tightly and fasten off, then join row ends. Turn right side out and stuff, then pull up the long end of yarn tightly, enclosing the stalk. Fasten off, then sew the stalk in place.

To shape the pumpkin into sections, thread the long end of yarn through a darning needle then take it around the outside and up through the centre of the pumpkin. Pull the yarn tightly, then repeat this seven more times, making the sections roughly equal in size. Fasten off.

Use black yarn to work a zig-zag line for the mouth. Work the eyes as for the scarecrow. Work short straight black stitches for the nose and eyebrows as shown in the illustration on page 99.

The pierrot

The body

Begin at lower edge and using white cast on 60 sts, marking the exact centre of the cast on row with a coloured thread.

1st row: (K 2 tog) to end – 30 sts.

Beginning with a K row, st-st 20 rows. Break off white and join on pink.

To shape the neck: *Next row:* K 6, (K 2 tog) 3 times, K 6, (K 2 tog) 3 times, K 6 – 24 sts.

St-st 10 rows.

Next row: (P 2 tog) to end – 12 sts. Break off yarn leaving a long end. Thread it through remaining sts, pull up tightly and fasten off.

The arms [make two alike]

Begin at top of arm and using white cast on 18 sts.

1st row: (P 2 tog) to end – 9 sts. Beginning with a K row, st-st 5 rows. Break off white and join on pink then st-st 3 rows. Break off yarn and finish off as for the body.

The hat

Using black cast on 30 sts then g-st 2 rows.

Break off black and join on white. Beginning with a K row, st-st 2 rows.

To shape top: *Next row:* (K 3, K 2 tog) to end – 24 sts.

St-st 3 rows.

Next row: (K 2, K 2 tog) to end – 18 sts.

St-st 3 rows.

Next row: (K 1, K 2 tog) to end – 12 sts.

St-st 3 rows. Break off yarn leaving a long end then thread it through remaining sts, pull up tightly and fasten off.

The collar

Using black cast on 120 sts. Break off black and join on white.

1st row: (K 2 tog) to end – 60 sts.

2nd row: (K 2 tog) to end – 30 sts. Beginning with a P row, st-st 3 rows then cast off.

The pom-pons [make four]

Wind a strand of black yarn 8 times around two fingers. Tie sewing thread very tightly around centres of strands. Trim yarn strands very short to make tiny pom-pons.

To make up the pierrot

Make up the body and arms and add facial features as for the ghost [see page 96].

For the hair cut a few 8 cm [3 in] lengths of tan yarn and sew them together at centres then sew to top of head. Fray out the yarn ends then space them out evenly all round the head.

Join the row ends of the hat, turn right side out and stuff the top. Place on pierrot's head and sew cast on edge in place. Sew two pom-pons to front of hat and trim the ends of hair.

Join row ends of the collar then sew cast off edge of collar to the last knitted row of white on the body. Sew the two remaining pom-pons to front of body. Using black yarn work a line of back stitches round each wrist, between the white and pink knitted rows.

Friar Tuck

The body

Begin at lower edge and using brown cast on 60 sts, marking the exact centre of the cast on row with a coloured thread.

1st row: (K 2 tog) to end – 30 sts.

Beginning with a K row, st-st 20 rows. Break off brown and join on pink.

To shape the neck: *Next row:* K 6, (K 2 tog) 3 times, K 6, (K 2 tog) 3 times, K 6 – 24 sts.

St-st 10 rows.

Next row: (P 2 tog) to end – 12 sts. Break off yarn leaving a long end. Thread it through remaining sts, pull up tightly and fasten off.

The arms [make two alike]

Begin at top of arm and using brown cast on 18 sts.

1st row: (P 2 tog) to end – 9 sts. Beginning with a K row, st-st 5 rows.

Break off brown and join on pink then st-st 3 rows. Break off yarn and finish off as for the body.

The hair

Begin at lower edge and using fawn cast on 26 sts.

Beginning with a P row, st-st 2 rows. Break off yarn leaving a long end. Thread this loosely through the sts and leave.

The collar

Using brown cast on 40 sts and st-st 3 rows then cast off.

The belt

Make a 22 cm [$8\frac{3}{4}$ in] long twisted cord using double fawn yarn. Knot the ends and trim close to knots.

To make up Friar Tuck

Make the body and arms and add facial features as for the ghost [see page 96].

Join row ends of the hair. Place it on the head and pull up the length of yarn threaded through the sts, to fit the head, leaving a bare patch at the top. Sew these sts and the cast on edge in place.

Join row ends of the collar. Place it round the neck as shown in the illustration, then sew cast on and cast off edges in place. Tie the belt round the waist and sew the knot to the body.

Robin Hood

The body

Begin at lower edge and using pale green cast on 60 sts marking the exact centre of the cast on row with a coloured thread.

1st row: (K 2 tog) to end – 30 sts.

Beginning with a K row, st-st 6 rows. Break off light green and join on dark green then st-st 4 rows.

Join on tan and st-st 2 rows. Break off tan and continuing in dark green, st-st 8 rows. Break off dark green and join on pink.
To shape the neck: *Next row:* K 6, (K 2 tog) 3 times, K 6, (K 2 tog) 3 times, K 6 – 24 sts.
St-st 10 rows.
Next row: (P 2 tog) to end – 12 sts. Break off yarn leaving a long end. Thread this through remaining sts, pull up tightly and fasten off.

The arms [make two alike]

Begin at top of arm and using dark green cast on 18 sts.
1st row: (P 2 tog) to end – 9 sts.
Beginning with a K row, st-st 5 rows. Break off dark green and join on pink then st-st 3 rows. Break off yarn and finish off as for the body.

The hat

Using light green cast on 26 sts and g-st 4 rows. Break off light green and join on dark green.
Beginning with a K row, st-st 2 rows.
Shape top: *1st row:* K 11, (K 2 tog) twice, K 11 – 24 sts.
2nd and every following alternate row: P.
3rd row: K 10, (K 2 tog) twice, K 10 – 22 sts.
5th row: K 9, (K 2 tog) twice, K 9 – 20 sts.
Next row: (P 2 tog) to end – 10 sts. Cast off.

The collar

Using light green cast on 36 sts and beginning with a K row, st-st 3 rows. Cast off K wise.

To make up Robin Hood

Make up the body and arms and add facial features as for the ghost [see page 96].

For the buckle work straight stitches in black on the tan rows at centre front of body, as shown in the illustration.

For the hair cut a few 8 cm [3 in] lengths of brown yarn and sew them together at centres then sew to top of head. Fray out the ends of yarn and space them out evenly all round the head. Join the row ends of the hat, then oversew across the cast off sts. Turn right side out and stuff lightly. Place the hat on the head tilting it slightly to one side. Sew the cast on edge in place. Sew a couple of loops of brown yarn to one side of hat above the light green portion for feathers. Trim ends of hair.

Oversew row ends of collar together. Place round the neck and sew cast off edge of collar to last knitted row of dark green on body. Sew cast on edge of collar in place also.

The cave-man

The body

Begin at lower edge and using tan cast on 60 sts, marking the exact centre of the cast on row with a coloured thread.
1st row: (K 2 tog) to end – 30 sts.
Beginning with a K row, st-st 12 rows. Break off tan and join on pink then st-st 8 rows.
To shape the neck: *Next row:* K6, (K 2 tog) 3 times, K 6, (K 2 tog) 3 times, K 6 – 24 sts.
St-st 10 rows.
Next row: (P 2 tog) to end – 12 sts. Break off yarn leaving a long end. Thread it through remaining sts, pull up tightly and fasten off.

The arms [make two alike]

Begin at top of arm and using pink cast on 18 sts.
1st row: (P 2 tog) to end – 9 sts.
Beginning with a K row, st-st 8 rows. Break off yarn and finish off as for the body.

The shoulder strap

Using tan cast on 34 sts. St-st 5 rows, decreasing 1 st at each end of every row – 24 sts. Cast off loosely.

The club

Using brown cast on 4 sts.
1st row: Inc K wise into every st – 8 sts.
St-st 10 rows.
Next row: (K1, inc in next st) to end – 12 sts.
St-st 6 rows. Break off yarn leaving a long end, thread it through sts, pull up tightly and fasten off.

To make up the cave-man

Make up the body and arms and add facial features as for the ghost [see page 96].

Place the shoulder strap over the left shoulder and sew the row ends to the last row of tan on the body as shown in the illustration.

For the hair cut a few 4 cm [$1\frac{1}{2}$ in] lengths of brown yarn and fray them out then sew them together at the centres. Sew to top of head and trim the ends.

Roll up the club across the width enclosing a little stuffing, then sew row ends in place. Using brown yarn, take stitches back and forth through the club pulling tightly, to give the club a nobbly appearance. Sew the club to the hand.

The fisherman

The body

Begin at lower edge and using yellow cast on 60 sts, marking the exact centre of the cast on edge with a coloured thread.

1st row: (K 2 tog) to end – 30 sts.

Beginning with a K row, st-st 20 rows. Break off yellow and join on pink.

To shape the neck: *Next row:* K 6, (K 2 tog) 3 times, K 6, (K 2 tog) 3 times, K 6 – 24 sts.

St-st 10 rows.

Next row: (P 2 tog) to end – 12 sts. Break off yarn leaving a long end. Thread it through remaining sts, pull up tightly and fasten off.

The arms [make two alike]

Begin at top of arm and using yellow cast on 18 sts.

1st row: (P 2 tog) to end – 9 sts. Beginning with a K row, st-st 5 rows. Break off yellow and join on pink then st-st 3 rows. Break off yarn and finish off as for the body.

The sou'wester hat

Begin at edge of brim and using yellow cast on 42 sts then g-st 6 rows.

To shape top: *Next row:* (K 1, K 2 tog) to end – 28 sts.

Beginning with a P row, st-st 3 rows.

Next row: (K 2, K 2 tog) to end – 21 sts.

St-st 3 rows.

Next row: (K 2 tog) to last st, K 1 – 11 sts.

Break off yarn leaving a long end, thread it through remaining sts, pull up tightly and fasten off.

The fish

Begin at tail end of fish and using silver cast on 10 sts.

St-st 12 rows.

Next row: (K 2 tog) to end – 5 sts. Break off yarn leaving a long end, thread it through remaining sts, pull up tightly and fasten off.

To make up the fisherman

Make up the body and arms and add facial features as for the ghost [see page 96].

Join the row ends of hat and turn right side out. Put a little stuffing in the top, then sew to the head through the first knitted row of shaping for the top.

Work four chain stitches in brown down the front of the body, for buttons.

Join the row ends of the fish, having the K side of the work outside. Turn right side out and stuff, then oversew across the cast on edge. Wind black sewing thread tightly round and round near to the tail end of the fish, then oversew round centre of tail to divide into two fins.

Work black stitches for the eyes and mouth, using sewing thread. Attach the fish to fisherman's hand with a loop of sewing thread.

The Roman

The body

Begin at lower edge and using white cast on 60 sts, marking the exact centre of the cast on row with a coloured thread.

1st row: (K 2 tog) to end – 30 sts.

Beginning with a K row, st-st 20 rows. Break off white and join on pink.

To shape the neck: *Next row:* K 6, (K 2 tog) 3 times, K 6, (K 2 tog) 3 times, K 6 – 24 sts.

St-st 10 rows.

Next row: (P 2 tog) to end – 12 sts. Break off yarn leaving a long end. Thread it through remaining sts, pull up tightly and fasten off.

The arms [make two alike]

Begin at top of arm and using white cast on 18 sts.

1st row: (P 2 tog) to end – 9 sts. Beginning with a K row, st-st 5 rows.

Break off white and join on pink then st-st 3 rows. Break off yarn and finish off as for the body.

The toga

Using white cast on 50 sts.

St-st 7 rows, decreasing 1 st at each end of every row – 36 sts. Cast off loosely K wise.

The hair

Using brown cast on 5 sts.

1st row: Inc K wise into every st – 10 sts.

2nd row: Inc K wise into every st – 20 sts.

G-st 8 rows. Break off yarn and fasten off the end. Thread a strand of yarn through the sts slipping them off the needle, then leave.

The laurel wreath

Cut three 25 cm [10 in] lengths of green yarn. Fold them in half and plait the six strands to make a 7 cm [$2\frac{3}{4}$ in] length. Tie sewing thread round and trim off yarn ends. Make another plait in the same way.

The scroll

Using fawn cast on 8 sts and st-st 11 rows. Cast off K wise.

To make up the Roman

Make up the body and arms and add facial features as for the ghost [see page 96].

Oversew the row ends of the hair together then gather up the cast on sts tightly and fasten off. Place the hair on the Roman's head. Pin each loose st to the head, pulling the sts downwards to stretch them. Draw the strand of yarn out of the sts, then sew each st to head removing the pins as you go.

Pin the laurel wreath plaits to the hair, crossing over the folded ends at the front and the other ends at the back. Sew plaits in place.

On the toga piece, use purple yarn to take small running stitches, down the row ends and just above the cast off edge. Place the toga over the left shoulder as shown in the illustration, with the cast on edge nearest to the neck. Sew the row ends of the toga in place, level with the cast on edge of the body and catching the ends of the cast on edge of the toga together.

Roll up the scroll tightly and tie a strand of red yarn around it. Sew scroll to the hand.

Santa Claus

The body

Begin at lower edge and using red cast on 60 sts, marking the exact centre of the cast on row with a coloured thread.

1st row: (K 2 tog) to end – 30 sts.

Beginning with a K row, st-st 8 rows. Join on black and st-st 4 rows.

Break off black and continuing in red, st-st 8 rows.

Break off red and join on pink.

To shape the neck: *Next row:* K 6, (K 2 tog) 3 times, K 6, (K 2 tog) 3 times, K 6 – 24 sts.

St-st 10 rows.

Next row: (P 2 tog) to end – 12 sts. Break off yarn leaving a long end. Thread it through remaining sts, pull up tightly and fasten off.

The arms [make two alike]

Begin at top of arm and using red cast on 18 sts.

1st row: (P 2 tog) to end – 9 sts.

Beginning with a K row, st-st 5 rows. Break off red and join on pink then st-st 3 rows. Break off yarn and finish off as for the body.

The beard

Using white cast on 12 sts.

1st row: Inc K wise into every st – 24 sts.

Now work in g-st, decreasing 1 st at each end of every row until 2 sts remain. Fasten off the 2 sts.

The sack

Using fawn cast on 10 sts and st-st 35 rows.
Cast off K wise.

The hat

Using white cast on 32 sts and g-st 2 rows. Break off white and join on red. Beginning with a K row, st-st 4 rows.
Shape the top: *Next row:* K 2 tog, (K 8, K 2 tog) 3 times – 28 sts.
St-st 3 rows.
Next row: K 1, K 2, tog, (K 6, K 2 tog) 3 times, K 1 – 24 sts.
St-st 3 rows.
Next row: (K 1, K 2 tog) to end – 16 sts.
St-st 3 rows.
Next row: (K 2 tog) to end – 8 sts.
Next row: P.
Next row: (K 2 tog) to end – 4 sts. Break off yarn leaving a long end. Thread this through remaining sts then pull up tightly and fasten off.

To make up Santa Claus

Make up the body and arms and add the eyes as for the ghost [see page 96]. Work a couple of stitches in red yarn for the nose. Sew the cast on edge of the beard to the face as shown in the illustration. Now work a V-shape on the beard in black yarn for the mouth, taking yarn through from back of head when doing this.

Oversew the row ends of the hat together then turn right side out. Make a small pom-pon from white yarn and sew it to top of hat. Put a little stuffing in the hat. Pin it on Santa's head, having the cast on edge level with the last row of red on the body at the back and above the eyes at the front. Place seam of hat at centre back also. Sew cast on edge in place.

Pull top of hat slightly over to one side and catch in place as shown in the illustration.

For the buckle work straight green stitches on the black rows at centre front of body.

Fold sack in half bringing cast on and cast off edges together. Oversew row ends together then turn right side out. Stuff the sack then tie a strand of green yarn round to hold stuffing in place. Sew the sack to Santa's hand as shown in the illustration.

The artist

The body

Begin at lower edge and using brown tweedy yarn cast on 60 sts, marking the exact centre of the cast on row with a coloured thread.

1st row: (K 2 tog) to end – 30 sts.

Beginning with a K row, st-st 4 rows. Break off brown and join on blue then st-st 16 rows. Break off blue and join on pink.

To shape the neck: *Next row:* K 6, (K 2 tog) 3 times, K 6, (K 2 tog) 3 times, K 6 – 24 sts.

St-st 10 rows.

Next row: (P 2 tog) to end – 12 sts. Break off yarn leaving a long end. Thread it through remaining sts, pull up tightly and fasten off.

The arms [make two alike]

Begin at top of arm and using blue cast on 18 sts.

1st row: (P 2 tog) to end – 9 sts.

Beginning with a K row, st-st 5 rows. Break off blue and join on pink then st-st 3 rows. Break off yarn and finish off as for the body.

The bow tie

Using orange cast on 40 sts and st-st 2 rows then cast off.

The beret

Using dark blue cast on 24 sts.

1st row: Inc K wise into every st – 48 sts.

Beginning with a P row, st-st 7 rows.

Shape the top: *Next row:* (K 1, K 2 tog) to end 32 sts.

Next row: P.

Next row: (K 2 tog) to end – 16 sts.

Next row: P.

Next row: (K 2 tog) to end – 8 sts. Break off yarn leaving a long end, thread it through remaining sts, pull up tightly and fasten off.

The palette

Using dark brown cast on 28 sts and st-st 4 rows.

Next row: (K 2 tog) to end – 14 sts.

Next row: (P 2 tog) to end – 7 sts. Cast off.

The brush

Using fawn, make a tightly twisted cord about 7 cm [2¾ in] in length from four strands of yarn. Wind and knot sewing thread tightly round and round the cord, 5 cm [2 in] away from the folded ends of the cord. Sew ends of thread into the cord. Fray out the ends of yarn beyond this point, for the brush bristles. Put a dab of glue on these ends and twist between finger and thumb to hold them together.

To stiffen the brush handle use a length of brown yarn and sew one end into the twisted cord just below the sewing thread. Wind the yarn tightly round the cord working towards the folded ends. Sew yarn to the cord at this end, then wind yarn back up the handle, winding it more closely as you go to make a tapered shape. Sew end of yarn into handle.

Finally, roll the handle under a warm iron to smooth it.

To make up the artist

Make up the body and arms and add facial features as for the ghost [see page 96].

Join row ends of the beret then use the long end of yarn to make a tiny twisted cord at centre top of beret. Pin beret to head, tilting it to one side as shown in the illustration. Tuck a few loops of yellow yarn inside the beret at front, for the hair. Sew the cast on edge of beret in place. Pull beret over to the side and catch in place.

Form the bow tie strip into a bow shape then sew a strand of matching yarn round the centre to hold in place. Sew bow to front of the artist, at the neck edge.

Bring row ends of the palette together then oversew across the cast off sts. Oversew the row ends together but leave the first two knitted rows of the palette open. Poke a small hole in the palette near to these two rows, then oversew round the hole to keep it open. Press the palette with a warm iron to flatten it. Now work a few stitches in various colours on the palette, for the paints.

Sew the palette to one hand and the brush to the other hand as shown in the illustration.

The cowboy

Note: The lowest portion of the cowboy's body is different from the other toys as it is knitted in reversed st-st, to resemble sheepskin chaps.

The body

Begin at lower edge and using white cast on 60 sts, marking the exact centre of the cast on row with a coloured thread.

1st row: (K 2 tog) to end – 30 sts.

Beginning with a P row, st-st 10 rows. Break off white and join on brown then beginning with a K row, st-st 2 rows.

Break off brown and join on blue then continue in st-st and work 8 rows.

Break off blue and join on pink.

To shape the neck: *Next row:* K 6, (K 2 tog) 3 times, K 6, (K 2 tog) 3 times, K 6 – 24 sts.

St-st 10 rows.

Next row: (P 2 tog) to end – 12 sts. Break off yarn leaving a long end. Thread it through remaining sts, pull up tightly and fasten off.

The arms [make two alike]

Begin at top of arm and using blue cast on 18 sts.

1st row: (P 2 tog) to end – 9 sts.

Beginning with a K row, st-st 5 rows. Break off blue and join on pink then st-st 3 rows. Break off yarn and finish off as for the body.

The neckerchief

Using red cast on 40 sts and work in g-st, casting off 9 sts at beginning of the next 4 rows and slipping the first st on each row. Break off yarn leaving a long end. Thread it through the 4 remaining sts, pull up tightly and fasten off.

The ten gallon hat

Begin at edge of brim and using fawn cast on 45 sts.

G-st 6 rows.

To shape top: *Next row:* (K 1, K 2 tog) to end – 30 sts.

Beginning with a P row, st-st 9 rows.

Next row: (K 1, K 2 tog) to end – 20 sts.

Next row: P.

Next row: (K 2 tog) to end – 10 sts. Break off yarn leaving a long end then thread it through remaining sts, pull up tightly and fasten off.

The rope

Cut a 150 cm [60 in] length of tan yarn and make a very tightly twisted cord from this single strand. Knot ends and trim off yarn close to knot.

To make up the cowboy

Make up the body and arms, and add facial features as for the ghost [see page 96].

Place the cast on edge of the neckerchief round the last row of blue on the body. Cross over the ends at one side and oversew them tightly together with sewing thread. Sew the cast on edge to neck.

For the buckle work straight yellow stitches on the brown rows at centre front of body as shown in the illustration. Sew a few loops of brown yarn to forehead to hang down just above the eyes, for the hair.

Oversew the row ends of the hat together and turn right side out. Stuff the top lightly. Use matching yarn to work small running stiches round the hat at inner edge of brim. Pull up the running stitches a little, so that the hat fits nicely on the head, then fasten off the ends of the yarn. For the hat band make a twisted cord from a single strand of brown yarn and sew it in place. Sew the hat to the head through the knitted row just below the hat band, tilting it to one side. Coil the rope round and round and sew it to the cowboy's hands.

Index

Page numbers in italics indicate illustrations

***Opposite**: Humpty-dumpty toys – instructions begin on page 47*